DISCREDITED

Power, Privilege, and Community College Transfer

Lauren Schudde
Huriya Jabbar

Harvard Education Press
Cambridge, Massachusetts

Paperback ISBN 9781682539040

Library of Congress Cataloging-in-Publication Data

Names: Schudde, Lauren, author. | Jabbar, Huriya, author.
Title: Discredited : power, privilege, and community college transfer / Lauren Schudde, Huriya Jabbar.
Description: Cambridge, Massachusetts : Harvard Education Press, [2024] | Includes bibliographical references and index.
Identifiers: LCCN 2024005635 | ISBN 9781682539040 (paperback)
Subjects: LCSH: Educational mobility—United States. | Community colleges—United States. | Students, Transfer of—United States. | Education, Higher—United States—Sociological aspects.
Classification: LCC LB2360 .S367 2024 | DDC 378.1/69140973—dc23/eng/20240403
LC record available at https://lccn.loc.gov/2024005635

Published by Harvard Education Press,
an imprint of the Harvard Education Publishing Group
Harvard Education Press
8 Story Street
Cambridge, MA 02138

Cover Design: Patrick Ciano

Cover Image: threespeedjones/iStock via Getty Images

The typefaces used in this book are Legacy Serif Std and Knockout.

DISCREDITED

*This book is dedicated to our families,
who supported us as we pushed this
project along despite various obstacles,
and to the staff and students at our
focal institutions, who continually
met with our research team
to share their experiences.*

CONTENTS

FOREWORD
by Kevin J. Dougherty
ix

INTRODUCTION
The Field of Transfer
1

CHAPTER 1
Shifting the Gaze: Moving from an Organizational to a Field-Level Perspective on College Transfer
23

CHAPTER 2
Privileged Positions Held by University Actors
45

CHAPTER 3
Implementers and Challengers in the Community College System
69

CHAPTER 4
Students as Implementers
91

CHAPTER 5
Shifting the Field of Transfer: Implications and Steps Forward
117

APPENDIX
133

NOTES
147

ACKNOWLEDGMENTS
169

ABOUT THE AUTHORS
171

INDEX
173

FOREWORD

This book is a very welcome addition to the research and policy literature on transfer from community colleges as well as the vicissitudes of such transfer. It expands powerfully on the sociological tradition of research on community colleges that dates back to the work of Burton Clark in the 1950s and 1960s and Jerome Karabel in the 1970s.[1] In particular, Schudde and Jabbar's book lays out an organizational field perspective that counters the tendency of scholarship on the difficulties of transfer to focus on deficiencies in the actions of community colleges or their students, while ignoring how those transfer difficulties are rooted in the structure of the higher education system and the larger society. In doing this, this book both consolidates and goes beyond past work on community college transfer and opens up new vistas for future research and policy.

In my following remarks, I first review two main threads of the book's argument: its analysis of breakdowns in the advising process for would-be transfer students and its organizational field explanation of the systemic origins of those breakdowns. I then draw out some research and policy questions that flow from the book's theoretical perspective, research findings, and policy recommendations that future researchers and policy makers should pursue.

Schudde and Jabbar provide a very careful analysis of where breakdowns occur in the dissemination of information regarding transfer. They note how such breakdowns are typically ascribed to deficiencies in community college operations (poor advising) or student behavior (poor information-seeking and decision-making). However, the authors argue that this ignores how poor advising and student confusion are rooted in university power to decide who is admitted and which courses can transfer for credit. It also ignores the fact that universities frequently change their admissions and credit-transfer rules and often do a poor job of communicating those new rules to community college advisors and students. As a result, Schudde and Jabbar question the effectiveness of repair efforts that focus simply on improving information provision without addressing the institutional isolation and power inequality involved in the relationship between universities and community colleges.

In analyzing the sources of breakdown in the transfer admission and credit-transfer process, this book continues the sociological tradition of applying organizational analysis to understanding the role and function of community colleges.[2] Brint and Karabel as well as Dougherty conceptualized community colleges as operating within an organizational field dominated by universities, business, and state officials, in which community colleges were organizationally separate from universities and occupied subordinate market and political positions.[3] Schudde and Jabbar build on and move beyond this interorganizational analysis by drawing on the theory of strategic action fields developed by Fligstein and McAdam.[4] This theory focuses on how—within organizational fields defined by shared understanding of what is at stake and what tactics are appropriate—some actors are dominant, able to set the values and rules that govern the actions of dominated actors. Applying this concept to transfer from community colleges, Schudde and Jabbar particularly highlight the dominant role of university personnel (faculty, administrators, admissions personnel) in determining which community college students are admitted to what programs and what community credits will count toward meeting university general education and major requirements. Meanwhile, community college personnel (particularly advisors) and would-be transfer students act as rule takers, implementing university-set rules and having little voice in what form they take. In the process of laying out these interorganizational relationships of domination, the authors develop illuminating typologies of community college actors (implementers mostly but also some rebels) and transfer students (resource curators, hesitants, system trusters, or disconnected).

The strength of a new perspective lies in how well it not only consolidates and extends previous research but also poses fruitful questions for the next generation of researchers and policy makers. Schudde and Jabbar's book shows this kind of strength. It lays out a theoretical perspective and array of research findings and policy recommendations that powerfully consolidate and extend previous research and pose several sets of questions that should be important to future researchers and policy makers. The first set of questions concerns the beliefs and interests of university faculty and administrators. As Schudde and Jabbar demonstrate, the decisions made by university faculty and administrators with regard to accepting transfer students and awarding credit for their community college courses are shaped by their concerns about upholding academic standards, preserving institutional autonomy, and avoiding standardization of curriculum. Because these beliefs and interests drive university admissions and transfer-credit policies, it is important that researchers continue probing what university faculty and administrators believe about "academic standards" and "university autonomy" and what interests those beliefs serve. Furthermore, to the degree these university beliefs and interests lead to actions hindering transfer credit, how much and in what ways can those beliefs and interests be modified?

Second, this book discusses the important role that state officials (coordinating boards, legislatures, governors) do play and could play in shaping transfer policy and practice. This suggests the importance of further investigating the key beliefs and interests of those state actors with respect to community college transfer. For example, to what degree do state officials agree with or diverge from university actors in their beliefs and interests with regard to transfer policy and practice? If there is substantial divergence, can this be leveraged to effect significant improvements in transfer policy and practice, while not significantly harming academic standards and university autonomy?

Finally, Schudde and Jabbar's analysis of the organizational impediments to good transfer advising and high-level student awareness implicitly points to the high cost we pay by providing students with a plethora of educational choices and yet relying on often inefficient information provision to ensure that the choices students make are beneficial to them. This points to the need to continue probing how to reduce the social costs of a high choice/poor information regime, whether by simplifying choices and providing students with much more structured guidance or by other means that manifest awareness of the structural impediments to smooth transfer.[5]

Schudde and Jabbar's book makes a major contribution to advancing our understanding of the impediments to effective transfer from community colleges. Its organizational field-based analysis helps us move beyond simplistic analyses of the vicissitudes of the transfer process that largely rely on blaming students or community college personnel. Moreover, their research findings and policy recommendations lay out fruitful avenues for the next generation of research studies and policy initiatives addressing the transfer process.

Kevin J. Dougherty
Professor Emeritus of Higher Education and Education Policy
Teachers College, Columbia University

INTRODUCTION

The Field of Transfer

We first met Teresa in her second semester of community college. She was nineteen years old at the time, a Latina who was raised in Texas, primarily by her grandmother; her long hair was dyed purple-gray. When we met, in an empty and pristine classroom lab in a newly constructed building on her campus, she described how attending college was "never an option" but always "a definite thing," a priority instilled in her by her family. In high school, however, she received a C in one course, which shaped her decision to initially attend a community college instead of a university. She believed that this would help her chances of admission to a university later because universities were "not going to look at the high school . . . they'll be looking at your college stuff." She anticipated that starting at a community college would get her where she wanted to go by giving her "time to fix [her] GPA for these intimidating schools to judge [her] on."

Despite intending to transfer, Teresa was confused about the steps she needed to take to do so. When "starting out" at the community college, she didn't know which classes to take and worried about "accidentally taking wrong classes, or taking classes that won't transfer." She relied heavily on her advisors at the community college to help her "decipher things" and select courses. Yet she wasn't sure about how many of her "core courses" or "basics" would transfer to a four-year university or whether they would apply to her major.

Over the six years of our study, we spoke with Teresa five times. By the fourth year, she had transferred to a regional university. It was then that she consulted with university staff and advisors and learned that she would lose several credits because they would not apply toward a degree in her major as she had expected. Because Teresa consulted only with community college advisors before transferring and not with staff at her transfer destination, she was confused throughout the transfer process and did not know how to anticipate credit transfer. She was exasperated by the lack of alignment between institutions, exclaiming, "These schools need to get together and have all these classes transfer to each other; it's super annoying that you may pay for a class that you will not be able to use in your next school!" In an ideal system, she explained, "all of the classes [would] just transfer under the same name," but, she lamented, apparently that only happened in a "fairytale land." She even speculated that the confusion was intentional, "a conspiracy to make you pay for things you don't need." The process left her defeated and, even more concerning, it slowed her anticipated time to a bachelor's degree.

Like Teresa, one-third of American college students begin their postsecondary education at a community college.[1] Unlike Teresa, however, students often do not transfer, even though many of them aspire to complete a bachelor's degree. The vast majority of community college students aim to transfer "vertically" to a baccalaureate-granting institution, but only one-third do.[2] Community colleges are part of complex public postsecondary systems, where institutions are connected only loosely; they largely operate independently, making coordination across institutions difficult.

As Teresa's case illustrates, the lack of coordination and alignment between institutions can lead to confusion, lost credits, and even cynicism about the intentions of community college and university staff (i.e., "a conspiracy"). Her story also shows how a singular focus on community colleges—while disregarding universities—is insufficient to understand the challenges of vertical transfer, which requires cross-institutional coordination, planning, and communication. Our book takes a broader institutional view while also illuminating the layered personnel operating within each context, their communication with students, and the replication of these dynamics across Texas's varied postsecondary system. In order to do that, we take a political-ecological approach grounded in six years of widely sourced data. We show that institutional staff who coordinate and support postsecondary transfer follow agreed-upon rules, norms, and procedures, and students navigate the rules to transfer between institutions. Understanding how community college students, staff, *and* university personnel interact requires researchers to examine the political-ecological contexts in which those interactions take place—a field perspective. Leveraging six years of data on transfer-intending community college students and the personnel that make up their support systems, we examine the broader ecology of this complex policy environment—the organizational structures, the existing policies, and the culture of state politics—and the experiences of students and staff that navigate vertical transfer in Texas.

Prior research, including recent contributions that highlight the "overt and hidden barriers" students experience while transferring, illustrates how students experience the process of transfer.[3] An organizational approach—one that captures not just the student experience but also the structures that shape it—is useful for further examining those barriers and how to intervene. Some sociological theories argue that community college actors, such as advisors, "cool out" student ambitions, diverting those who might otherwise earn a baccalaureate.[4] Recent counterarguments shift the focus and describe inadequate structures in community colleges, which lack sufficient supports to keep students on track toward a degree.[5] Despite recent attention to community college structure, research aimed at understanding why so few community college entrants earn a bachelor's degree overlooks critical components of the broader ecological contexts that shape transfer, especially the related politics and the interactions between institutions that ultimately shape the field of transfer in ways that can either expand or undermine access to universities.

Although prior scholars have shown how community colleges can develop and improve support services for students, truly transforming transfer requires moving beyond this narrow focus. Student experiences must be understood within a larger context. To illuminate how and under what conditions students successfully navigate transfer, we must examine the broader environment—the interorganizational dynamics among an extended set of actors across community colleges, universities, and state agencies. Without a clear view of the transfer field as a whole, which extends far beyond community college institutions, we cannot fully comprehend the sources and extent of confusion experienced by students (and sometimes advisors) who are navigating transfer, or how to intervene effectively.

To understand the power dynamics and roles of actors in the transfer system, we focus our inquiry on transfer-related college personnel and transfer-intending students in Texas. Texas educates 13 percent of the country's community college students; community colleges serve as an entryway to higher education for 40 percent of college students in the state.[6] Higher education institutions in the state developed locally, rather than as a holistic system planned by state government, and historically prioritize institutional autonomy.[7] Although the Texas higher education context has some unique features, it can offer lessons to many other community college contexts.

Policy Landscape of Community College Transfer

The community college pathway to a baccalaureate appeals to both policy makers and students as a low-cost alternative to the first two years at a four-year college. In practice, however, there are several stages in the transfer process at which transfer-intending students face challenges: the early period of college, when some students fall behind academically; the transition (including application and enrollment) from a two-year to a four-year college;[8] and the period after transitioning to a new institution.[9] Credit loss is a particularly salient problem facing transfer-intending students, and it looms across the different phases of transfer, which are intricately connected. Although students may not be cognizant of credit loss until after they move to a baccalaureate-granting institution (or, at the least, until they apply to universities and examine how credits will move between institutions), the problem begins with the accumulation of unnecessary coursework early in college.[10]

The process of postsecondary transfer is fraught with bureaucratic hurdles and complex information. Students who intend to transfer must navigate requirements at both their current college and their prospective destination. Key barriers to transfer include opaque transfer policies, bureaucratic hurdles, inadequate information about credit portability, and support services that are insufficient for maintaining progress.[11] Although we focus on transfer from community colleges to baccalaureate-granting universities, not all transfer is "vertical."[12] Many students, including those we will talk about in this book, transfer between universities, or between community colleges—"swirling" among institutions.[13]

States use several policies to improve the transferability of credits and the clarity of transfer information, including a transferable core curriculum, statewide articulation agreements, common course numbering, and reverse transfer policies. The most common state transfer policy is a transferable core of lower-division courses, a set of lower-division courses that provide breadth of knowledge and are universally accepted at public colleges. Three-quarters of states—including Texas, where we focus our inquiry—have adopted this strategy, which should standardize recommended courses for transfer, thereby creating a clear transfer pathway.[14] Although core curricula, including in Texas, typically include general education coursework that should overlap with premajor and major baccalaureate requirements and thereby create a clear transfer pathway, in practice, lower-division requirements can vary by major. In Texas and in some other states, like Ohio, where individual institutions decide which courses fulfill component areas of the core curriculum, students can accrue core credits that may not ultimately apply toward their degree in a given program.[15]

People often assume that transfer students follow a "two plus two" model, where they complete two years at a community college, and then two years at a university, resulting in a degree in four years. Yet some states do not have a clear policy that supports a "two plus two" program for students.[16] Most states have some form of statewide transfer agreements (also called articulation agreements) that focus on preventing credit loss for students moving between institutions.[17] Over two-thirds of states hold guaranteed articulation agreements, in which associate degrees are fully transferable for junior status at a public university; other states, including Texas, however, still rely on "bilateral agreements" between two institutions.[18] These bilateral agreements are decentralized; they offer greater institutional autonomy, as they can be tailored to institutional preferences and don't require approval from the state. Even when statewide agreements are present, departments often must rely on bilateral agreements between institutions to negotiate how credits will apply toward a bachelor's degree, given variation in postsecondary curricula.[19] On their own, however, stand-alone bilateral agreements (without additional state transfer policies) leave students and advisors to navigate specific agreements between colleges and programs, which can contribute to misaligned information across various sources.[20]

Just under half of all states, including Texas, use policies like common course numbering and reverse transfer to further facilitate transfer and degree attainment.[21] Under common course numbering systems, public postsecondary institutions use uniform numbering conventions for lower-division courses, which make it easier for students to know how a course at one institution translates to the curriculum in another program. In Texas, the common course-numbering system is mandatory for public two-year colleges and optional for universities. For that reason, transfer-intending students have to translate course numbers from two-year colleges into their university equivalents to understand how course credits will count toward their desired degree upon transfer, an additional burden placed on students. This is another case in which the policy prioritizes institutional autonomy for universities and thus undermines the effectiveness of the system. Texas also has a mandate for reverse transfer. States that have reverse credit transfer policies enable students to earn an associate degree posttransfer after completing additional associate degree requirements at their baccalaureate-granting institution.[22] Common course numbers and reverse transfer policies are somewhat less common than statewide transfer agreements: both policies are used by twenty-two states.[23] There is little evidence about their effectiveness or the extent to which they clarify the transfer process for students and advisors.

In contexts like Texas that have institution-driven transfer policies, universities have considerable power over which previously acquired credits apply toward a degree. In these contexts, associate degrees and bachelor's degrees are often not "stackable"—the requirements for the shorter-term degree do not align with those for a longer-term degree in the same field.[24] That is, even if students earn at least sixty credits to receive an associate degree, not all of those credits apply toward a bachelor's degree in the same major. Because degrees from different institutions have different lower-division requirements, students who earn a pretransfer associate degree report, posttransfer, feeling surprised when credits do not apply toward their major.[25] These issues likely add length to the amount of time students take to earn a bachelor's degree. Nationally, the majority of students (55.9 percent) take longer than four years to complete a bachelor's degree, but transfer can dramatically increase time to degree.[26]

Texas Public Higher Education Context

Texas is the second most populous state in the country, and its population is rapidly expanding.[27] That population is also among the most diverse: Latinos make up 39 percent of Texas's people—more than double their proportion nationally—probably because of the state's geographic proximity to and historical ties with Mexico, which lies along Texas's southern border.[28] Given the size and geographic and cultural diversity of the state, it's not surprising that postsecondary education institutions developed locally, resulting in a largely decentralized higher education system.

The Texas public higher education "system"—which is technically not a system but rather a loosely connected group of smaller systems and districts—now includes seventy-four two-year institutions (some of which are independent community colleges and others of which are campuses within broader districts) and thirty-seven four-year institutions, including a number of different college and university systems with their own chancellors (at the system level), presidents (at the institution level), and governing boards.[29] This arrangement is distinct from that in states like California, which formed under the state's "master plan" for higher education, and in other states that have statewide systems of higher education institutions. Even in more centralized higher education systems, institutional actors negotiate over how to navigate credit transfer and implement transfer agreements, processes that are amplified in the Texas context because of its decentralized higher education structure and emphasis on local control.

The Texas Higher Education Coordinating Board (referred to as THECB or *coordinating board* from here on) was established in 1955 with the goal of coordinating all these institutions that make up the public higher education pipeline for transfer.[30] Although the coordinating board is a governor-appointed public agency with regulatory powers, its authority does not supersede that of institutional or system governing boards. Historically, college and university leaders in the state emphasized institutional autonomy and resisted some of the coordinating board's efforts, such as recent attempts to expand statewide transfer agreements in specific fields of study.[31] The state's geographic, demographic, and institutional diversity, coupled with a state culture that historically prioritized local control and minimal regulation, also present challenges to coordination.[32] The push and pull among the coordinating board, the legislature, and the individual systems and institutions creates ongoing tension.

Texas exemplifies an institution-driven transfer system, where decisions about credit applicability and fulfilling major requirements are determined by individual institutions.[33] The decentralized nature of transfer in Texas means these requirements can vary for each prospective institution, and the state has not sought to build statewide transfer agreements (e.g., offering associate degrees guaranteed to transfer and apply toward a bachelor's degree in the same field), which we see in many other states. Eighty-one percent of Texas community college students enroll in transfer programs; yet less than one-third of students transfer to a university within six years, a pattern that closely mirrors national trends.[34] The low attainment of transfer goals reflects the bureaucratic hurdles and complex information students must navigate to transfer. Students who intend to transfer must understand both the requirements of their current college and those of their prospective destination institution.

The various intersecting policies and the frequently shifting state transfer initiatives illustrate the dynamic nature of higher education transfer policy directives, in which personnel struggle to keep up with new foci and terminology intended to solve the transfer problem. As we will describe in further detail, some personnel acknowledge being out of touch with current policies because of fluctuations in policy directives (along with limited communication about those directives) and the fact that mandates, like the core curriculum, appear to be, in the word of one community college administrator we spoke to, "unmanned." Each initiative has little money or accountability behind it, which allows the winds to shift quickly from one to the next: this means there is typically little enforcement of the policies.

Texas Compared with Other States

Although Texas's postsecondary context is unique in its size and history, other states that similarly rely on institution-driven or credit equivalency transfer systems also require students and advising staff to customize student pathways from various transfer guides. Indeed, two-thirds of states allow institutional autonomy over how premajor credits transfer.[35] Decentralized transfer systems, in which each institution determines whether and how to build transfer partnerships and provide transfer information, place the burden on students and advisors to familiarize themselves with transfer options. Transfer processes are incredibly complex for students who need to compare and contrast several different transfer options that include various majors and prospective universities. Even in states that use more transparent "two plus two" systems, institutional actors often must discern how credits from one college apply toward a degree at the destination college.[36]

Given its multiple public university and community college systems, the Texas higher education context may be more decentralized than that in other states. The issue of misalignment between policy signals from different institutions—where universities and community colleges sometimes emphasize different policies or differentially encourage adopting versus adapting/combining the policies—may be a result of the state's macro context, which prioritizes local control and institutional autonomy. However, the extant literature on community college transfer suggests that these issues are not unique to Texas. Research on effective transfer partnerships emphasizes the importance of well-articulated transfer curricula and outreach among staff at four-year institutions to clarify whether and how they accept credits upon transfer, even in contexts that have statewide transfer agreements.[37] Our research directly examines how students juggle and make sense of competing information from different institutions and the role college personnel play in creating and resolving conflicting transfer policy information. Understanding students' experiences with navigating transfer—and the role that college personnel at sending and receiving institutions play in shaping those experiences—has implications for state contexts beyond that of Texas.

Role of Institutional Actors in Community College Transfer and Policy Reform

Students require clarity, early in their college career, about how coursework will transfer *and* apply toward a desired degree, but it is often left to individual institutions to offer that information.[38] Although state-level policies may structure the way public institutions determine credit transfer, they do not guarantee that institutions will pass along relevant transfer policy information to students clearly and coherently. Students' transfer pathways are deeply entangled with how institutions distill and disseminate information about credit portability.[39] The information students obtain from transfer personnel and institutional websites is filtered by institutional actors who implement transfer. Students typically access transfer information and support services that colleges offer them *after* state and institutional policies are interpreted by institutional actors.[40]

Without sufficient staff support, students struggle to find information about whether and how credits will transfer; many transfer students—like Teresa—are later surprised when credits fail to transfer or don't apply toward a degree.[41] Although most college websites offer institutional and program-specific information, many do not provide clear or consistent information about transfer.[42] Information barriers may have important repercussions for students, including failure to transfer and, among those who transfer, credit loss and increased time to a baccalaureate.[43]

When institutions fail to provide adequate or consistent transfer information, students must seek it out—whether from "trusted others," such as friends and families, or from various websites—and determine which sources seem the most credible.[44] Noninstitutional contacts can help students navigate bureaucratic hurdles and gather information that "facilitates action" toward their educational aspirations, but only if students have this social capital.[45]

In the past two decades, scholars emphasized structuralist perspectives, which focus on the internal organization of institutions, to highlight how community colleges can improve support services for students. Most prior research, including the structural approach, has not examined institutional transfer as a *field*, where actors from multiple organizations, including community college advisors, university admissions personnel, and other staff, interact with each other and with students. Extant research on transfer focuses on structures in the community college itself and not on the pressures, messages, and interactions present in the broader environment in which the organization is embedded. In the case of transfer, students and transfer-related personnel interact within a much broader context: a complex higher education system where institutions are tenuously linked and individual colleges defend their autonomy.[46] State contexts—and stakeholders' interests—determine colleges' missions, the programs they offer, how they are funded, and what we expect of them.[47]

Transfer processes are complicated by these broader structures. Tensions arise as individual colleges seek their own goals and enact their own procedures for transfer, with little regard for other institutions and the needs of students.[48] Implicit in many faculty discussions and debates about course transfer are the assumptions that the quality of instruction and learning is lower in a community college setting, and that transfer students are academically underprepared. It is true, of course, that community colleges, as open-access institutions, accept students regardless of their K–12 experiences, but it is not clear that instructional quality is lower in community colleges than in universities. In fact, with their smaller class sizes, community colleges might offer more engaging learning contexts. These assumptions, informed by race- and class-based biases, as well as by the perceived hierarchies in higher education, often shape transfer policy and the willingness of university actors to develop more streamlined pathways, as our work will reveal. As a result, these incorrect assumptions can lead to ineffective, inefficient, and inequitable transfer policies.

Both advisors and students are left to navigate the complicated information structures and misaligned policies that result. The misalignment in policies is often the result of power dynamics and gatekeeping at selective—that is, noninclusive universities—that stymie more concrete and systematic policies to address transfer challenges. The complexity of the policy landscape then, in turn, requires students to gather more information and be proactive, placing the burden on the least powerful actors in the system. Transfer rules and regulations also shape the occupational identities of those who operate within them, including the support staff who manager and interpret state and institutional policies.[49] Examining that context and how students and staff interact with each other in this landscape can offer greater insights into the challenges community college students face in attaining their educational goals and can inform the steps reformers must take to transform transfer.

Mapping the Field of Transfer

Drawing on interviews from transfer personnel at community colleges and universities in Texas and longitudinal data from transfer-intending community college students, we build a field-level understanding of institutional transfer. Over the course of six years (beginning in fall 2015), we interviewed and followed 104 transfer-intending community college students who attended one of two public community college districts—Central Community College (CCC) and Fernando Community College System (FCCS) (these are pseudonyms)—in the same geographic region of Texas. CCC was a multicampus community college system in a metropolitan area and enrolled over forty thousand students each year, almost a quarter of whom received Pell Grants and just under half identified as White.[50] Many CCC students aimed to transfer to the local public university, which is among the most selective universities in the state. FCCS was a multicollege system in which Hispanic students constituted the racial/ethnic majority.[51] Most FCCS students aimed to transfer, with many entering broad-access public universities in the same city as FCCS. In addition to interviewing students annually for six years, we also interviewed transfer-relevant community-college and university personnel at the beginning and the end of the study to understand institutional policies and practices, along with staff perspectives on the transfer process.

To understand transfer at a field-level, we focus on how institutional actors develop and enact common understandings about the purpose, rules, and relationships in the transfer process.[52] This approach helps us uncover how institutional actors across levels of the higher education system work to determine credit-transfer policies and disseminate information, and how students navigate complex and constantly shifting transfer requirements. We highlight the varied ways that personnel at public universities create barriers to transfer through bureaucratic decisions, which shape the admissions and credit transfer processes and have important repercussions for transfer-intending community college students.

By emphasizing the transfer field, we argue for a shift from viewing community college transfer as a *community college* problem (the status quo in the literature and in policy discussions) to viewing it as a *public higher education* problem, illuminating how an interconnected web of institutional actors from many different positions across higher education institutions ultimately shape community college's transfer function. In doing so, we expand the cast of characters understood as responsible for transfer outcomes, including actors both within and outside of community college settings. Elucidating the ecology and politics of transfer is a necessary starting point for making effective changes to policy and practice. When scholars and policy makers focus too narrowly on the failures of structures *within* community colleges, they ignore the other powerful players and interests (e.g., university faculty) that shape the environments in which community college staff operate. Meaningful changes will require engaging a broader set of actors and getting them on board—actors who have often thwarted policies that could improve equity and access in the transfer field.

First, we argue that transfer needs to be examined at a field level. In chapter 1, "Shifting the Gaze: Moving from an Organizational to a Field-Level Perspective on College Transfer," we describe how our approach builds upon and extends existing research on community colleges and institutional transfer. We synthesize the scholarly research on community college transfer for the past five decades, including the literature on common barriers to transfer and challenges faced in improving transfer policies. We introduce our theoretical framework: strategic action fields, an organizational theory illuminating how actors build and maintain rules and norms in an existing power structure where there are dominant and nondominant (or dominated) actors, to understand the role of political-ecological contexts in vertical transfer.

In the next section of the book, we illustrate how institutional transfer functions as a strategic action field—and explore the lessons offered from this framing—by documenting how institutional and student actors interact to create, maintain, and respond to rules in the transfer field. Chapter 2, "Privileged Positions Held by University Actors," examines the roles and actions of university personnel. In this chapter, we draw on interviews with faculty and staff at four-year institutions that were common transfer destinations among students in our two community college districts. We distinguish between the various types of universities (e.g., flagship institutions, regional comprehensive institutions) and examine how institutional actors interact in the community college transfer field. We argue that university administrators, faculty, and staff hold dominant positions in the field, with the flagship universities holding outsized influence. Presenting evidence from two waves of interviews, we illustrate how, to maintain curricular autonomy, university administrators and faculty at state flagship schools fought against state transfer policies. University personnel set the rules and norms for credit transfer and applicability by setting standards for admission to programs, determining curricula and how credits transfer and apply to degree requirements, and facilitating (or thwarting) the development of transfer agreements. Given their power, university personnel worked to ensure that transfer mechanisms would benefit four-year institutions rather than broad-access community colleges. We argue that these patterns make it challenging for students to navigate transfer and for community colleges to support them.

Next, we shift to explore the nondominant actors in the transfer landscape, drawing on interview data with administrators and transfer services personnel. In chapter 3, "Implementers and Challengers in the Community College System," we first describe how some community college personnel voiced frustration about the field disadvantaging transfer-intending community college students. These personnel sought to challenge the status quo, and we outline their varied efforts to implement reforms. Most community college actors, however, were "implementers" who accepted the field as it was. They emphasized that existing transfer rules and norms serve to improve transfer success and highlighted that students' primary role is to inform themselves. Because most transfer personnel serve as implementers, we argue that community college staff ultimately reinforced the social order by maintaining the rules and norms set by universities.

We then turn to examine how students respond to the rules and norms of the transfer field in chapter 4, "Students as Implementers." Drawing on six years of interviews, we describe how students navigate the decentralized and complex transfer landscape. Students had little power, and they were often reliant on other actors to understand the intersecting policies and requirements for transfer. They believed that it was their responsibility to gather transfer information and sort through conflicting messages from staff at community colleges and universities. We argue that the decentralized nature of the higher education system and the variation in transfer information provided across institutions place the burden on students to familiarize themselves with transfer options. Through our analyses of these rich longitudinal data, we show that the complex structure of information—wherein each institution provides its own transfer information and resources, with little collaboration and minimal alignment between them—systematically disadvantages community college students. This arrangement ultimately undermines the democratic aims of community colleges, and it disproportionately affects low-income students and students of color, who are more likely to enter higher education through a community college.

After laying out the roles, implications, and consequences of the field, in chapter 5, "Shifting the Field of Transfer: Implications and Steps Forward," we consider next steps for policy and practice. We summarize the key challenges, describing how the status quo undermines equity and access in higher education, and we offer a path forward toward improved transfer for students and suggest a compromise for institutions and policy makers, both in Texas and in other states. Overall, our work illustrates complexities in the current transfer ecosystem, where different actors have different levels of information and power, and describes the repercussions of those inequities for student experiences and outcomes. Reframing institutional transfer in the context of field theory is a paradigm shift because doing so recasts the nonoptimal transfer function of community colleges from a "community college problem" to a "public higher education problem." Researchers and policy makers need to attend to political dynamics and power in college transfer. Our approach lays bare the true and underlying conflicts that have so far limited the potential of community colleges to broaden access to baccalaureate pathways. We leverage new evidence to point to solutions and concrete policies that can get to the root of the problem and encourage public higher education institutions to take shared responsibility for college transfer, and, ultimately, transform the field.

CHAPTER 1

Shifting the Gaze

Moving from an Organizational to a Field-Level Perspective on College Transfer

Community colleges play an important democratizing role by providing open access to postsecondary education for historically disadvantaged students.[1] Yet critics argue that community colleges also divert students, in part because they have high attrition rates and complex structures, making it difficult for students to navigate course, degree, and transfer requirements.[2] A recent meta-analysis of existing research suggests that entering a community college rather than a baccalaureate-granting institution decreases a student's probability of earning a bachelor's degree by 23 percentage points.[3] Overall, community colleges are "contradictory" institutions that both broaden access to higher education and make obtaining a degree more difficult for community college students because of inefficiencies in the transfer process.[4]

Postsecondary outcomes are influenced by a mix of individual factors, such as the position of students in the broader society (e.g., race, class, family education, or geography) and institutional characteristics of the institutions they attend (e.g., enrollment size, financial resources, student services). Most research on community college transfer emphasizes how individual or within-institution factors, including variation in transfer trajectories across student background and the presence of support services and bureaucratic hurdles within the institution, shape students' educational attainment. But community colleges do not exist in a vacuum: the experiences and opportunities of students are shaped by policy makers and institutional actors outside the community college walls. We need to examine how institutional actors in the broader postsecondary system interact to shape students' opportunities and transfer trajectories. Such efforts require shifting the focus to the *field* of transfer, recognizing that institutional actors and students operate within this broader system.

In this chapter, we synthesize the existing research on community colleges, including the literature on common barriers to transfer and transfer policies that can help overcome them, and provide an overview of the landscape. We consider what makes transferring from community colleges to universities so difficult. Since early investigations into how community colleges shape student outcomes, research has explored how and why the community college pathway to a bachelor's degree is more cumbersome than the pathway to the same degree at an institution that grants bachelor's degrees. Earlier theories argued that the mission of community colleges was at least partly to placate students by offering alternative credentials to a bachelor's degree, while more recent scholarly research acknowledges the varied goals of community colleges and their students.[5] A subset of community college research has examined the factors that predict vertical transfer, including student and institutional characteristics.[6] Drawing from those findings and taking a closer look at community colleges as organizations, the recent structural argument, presented by sociologists, attributes low rates of vertical transfer among community college baccalaureate aspirants to inadequate support services at community colleges, including advising and other structural supports for students, which make it difficult for students to reach their educational goals.

We illustrate how extant research hints at—but largely overlooks—the broader ecology of transfer. We then introduce the theoretical framework we used to adjust our gaze toward transfer at the field level.

Sorting Processes in Community Colleges: Understanding Diversion

Dating back several decades, theorists understood low rates of vertical transfer among community college entrants as an exercise of purposeful diversion. In his "cooling-out" hypothesis, Clark theorized that community college personnel impede students' aspirations toward a bachelor's degree by offering "substitute avenues" for success (i.e., terminal two-year degrees).[7] Brint and Karabel elaborated on Clark's theory, arguing that, through this "management of ambitions," community colleges divert students from their baccalaureate aspirations and buffer baccalaureate colleges from an influx of students seeking a degree.[8] In both arguments, community college actors relay these messages, which assumes either collusion with university actors or a coherent higher education system in which actors in different institutional sectors understand their roles in service to gatekeeping for bachelor's degrees.

Recent scholarship is skeptical of explicit diversionary efforts on the behalf of community college staff (i.e., community college personnel are not, in fact, purposefully diverting students away from their desired baccalaureate), but evidence confirms that entering a community, compared with a university, lowers a student's probability of earning a bachelor's degree.[9] Diversionary processes likely vary across student subgroups, contributing to inequities in transfer outcomes. Community colleges with student populations that are younger and more affluent and that have stronger academic preparation have higher transfer rates.[10] At the individual level, women, students with dependents, or those enrolled in a certificate program (rather than a degree program) appear less likely to transfer than their peers.[11] The cooling-out hypothesis suggests that institutional actors at community colleges contribute to unequal outcomes by funneling students with a lower probability of success (e.g., low-income students, students with dependents) toward tracks that are less likely to lead to transfer (e.g., certificate programs). Recent research, however, suggests that most community college students do not downwardly shift their degree aspirations—their aspirations actually "hold steady" over time.[12] At the same time, despite baccalaureate aspirations, many community college students do not transfer.

Structuralist theories of higher education argue that low rates of transfer are not, in fact, driven by purposeful diversion by staff but by community colleges' lack of support services, curricular structure, and clear guidance for students in navigating bureaucratic hurdles and dealing with conflicting demands.[13] Structuralists contend that transparent information, student support services, and ongoing assessments of students' college milestones can effectively move students toward their educational goals.[14] Without those structures, community college students interested in earning a bachelor's degree may be confused about how to start the transfer process or may fall off track unknowingly. Transfer-intending students must learn and navigate a "hidden curriculum" comprising taken-for-granted knowledge about how to proceed through the transfer process.[15]

Unequal Access to the "Hidden Curriculum" of Transfer

Transfer involves a series of bureaucratic procedures and hurdles that make it challenging for students to navigate the transfer process without sufficient support.[16] Transfer-intending students may struggle to track down necessary information, as "information about course content and prerequisites is often located in one place, while course schedules are in another place, and the requirements for specific degree programs are spelled out in yet another."[17] In her recent book, Wang described the "granular precision" necessary for transfer-intending community college students to access transferable courses or programs at the time when they need them because of both a lack of broad articulation and a "limited menu" of transferrable courses—a limited menu that is determined by university faculty and upheld by university staff.[18] To avoid "curricular friction," in which students accumulate unnecessary courses or are unable to get the transferable course they need, several pieces of students' academic and nonacademic lives must concurrently align, including "accurate information, money, schedule, [and] work."[19]

Not all students gain access to the hidden transfer curriculum. Navigating transfer requires drawing upon information from relationships and "social know-how," which are not evenly distributed.[20] Privileged forms of social capital—networks and relationships—and cultural capital—knowledge and behaviors relevant to navigating college—often increase access to strategic and procedural information about navigating credit transfer, program selection, and applications.[21] Yet community colleges disproportionately enroll nontraditional college students, including those who are older, have dependents, work full time or part time, and have external commitments that compete with schooling—students who are less likely to have those privileged forms of capital.[22] Most community college students are the first in their families to attend college, limiting their exposure to information about postsecondary bureaucratic processes compared with peers whose parents or close relatives attended college.[23]

Students seek, but struggle to obtain, accurate transfer information through advising or elaborate information gathering.[24] The hidden curriculum for transfer is overseen by staff.[25] Advisors and other support services staff determine how and when—if ever—to provide vital information pertinent to students' educational goals.[26]

Transfer-intending students must navigate requirements for both their current college and their prospective destination institution, which often requires engaging with personnel and published information at both institutions. When colleges send mixed signals or neglect to provide information about transfer requirements, it makes it difficult for students to navigate transfer pathways.[27] In the absence of adequate or consistent transfer information from their institution, students must seek information from several sources, including staff, "trusted others" such as friends and families, and various institutional websites, and they must deliberate over which sources seem most credible.[28] This complex process can result in a loss of time and money and, ultimately, movement away from the credential that students hope to earn.[29]

The structural argument attributes information constraints among community college students to structural problems within community colleges, including that the colleges are not adequately resourced to provide the individual advising necessary for navigating an environment with complex transfer agreements (which often vary by destination institution and major). In recent years, research has focused increasingly on the structure and supports available at community colleges and how they can be leveraged to overcome barriers and improve outcomes in the transfer process.

Illuminating the "Hidden Curriculum" of Transfer Through Scaffolding and Support

Many interventions at community colleges are aimed at improving the quality of transfer information and guidance available to students in an effort to illuminate the hidden curriculum of transfer. Community college personnel are one means by which vital information about transfer is disseminated. By introducing students to transfer guides or structured "maps," advising staff can guide movement from one institution to another. Making available clear, up-to-date information about transfer options helps students overcome informational barriers to transfer, as does "intrusive advising"—proactive advising that regularly checks in with students to assess progress.[30] Some institutions offer specialized services to guide transfer-intending students, including transfer-specific advisors, centers, and events, but the quality and availability of those resources vary.[31] Many community colleges cannot meet the demand for effective transfer advising.

Students' transfer pathways are deeply entangled with how institutions distill and disseminate information about credit portability.[32] To effectively navigate transfer, many students need greater support than most community colleges provide.[33] Having limited advising resources makes online information about transfer important, yet many community colleges offer little to no online content, and what is available is often confusing and out of date.[34] The U.S. Government Accountability Office, in a recent report on institutional transfer, found that the availability of clear transfer information varied dramatically across institutions.[35] This variation creates an uneven playing field, as students who attend colleges with opaque transfer information may struggle when attempting to transfer. The information students obtain from institutional agents and on institutional websites is filtered by institutions—students see only the transfer policies and support services that colleges share with them.[36]

State-level policies may structure how public institutions determine whether credits will transfer. Some states use strategies like common course numbering (universal course numbers across public institutions), a statewide core curriculum (a set of block of premajor coursework universally accepted at public institutions), and transfer articulation agreements (agreements articulating how credits will transfer across institutions/programs).[37] Although all of these policies aim to improve credit transfer and application, they do not guarantee that institutional actors will pass along relevant transfer information to students in a clear and coherent manner. In fact, personnel may experience conflicting incentives for supporting state policies toward transfer transparency and, like students, must also manage confusing and unclear signals about transfer. Despite attempts at both the state and institutional level to improve transfer information for community college students, these efforts often overlook that universities play a significant role in determining which students can transfer, whether and how transfer-aspirants receive accurate information, and how students' prior credits ultimately apply toward a given bachelor's degree.

The Underexamined Influence of Universities on the Transfer Process

Much of the prior research on improving transfer focuses on structures and constraints at community colleges. Yet, powerful university actors shape the infrastructure (e.g., information, transfer agreements) and the processes (e.g., recruitment, admissions, articulation) necessary to support vertical transfer. Many of the key barriers to transfer, including opaque transfer policies, complex bureaucratic processes, and inadequate information about credit portability, are deeply influenced by universities.[38]

Transfer-intending students often experience confusion about how to select courses and degrees, especially given their desire to avoid credit loss when they transfer.[39] They turn to actors at their community colleges for guidance but are often met with insufficient support services and out-of-date information. University actors have more up-to-date information but don't typically offer prospective transfer students guidance on pretransfer course taking. Instead, students primarily interact with admissions officers at universities closer to their application date, when they often receive generic guidance that is not applicable to their specific needs or, at times, information—especially about credit transfer and major requirements—that conflicts with what they learned from their community college.[40]

Many credit transfer decisions and major course requirements are determined by university actors, typically (though sometimes indirectly) by faculty who determine program curricula. Faculty and administrators at less-inclusive institutions—universities deemed "selective" that do not rely on transfer students for enrollment management—seek to preserve their institution's prestige and selectivity. Among faculty and staff at these less inclusive institutions, (mis)conceptions about transfer students can manifest through an emphasis on rigor or concerns about accepting courses from other institutions and serve as a hindrance to building a transfer-receptive institutional culture.[41] Negative perceptions of transfer have negative repercussions for students—universities without transfer-receptive cultures appear to contribute to poor transfer outcomes for community college students.[42]

Though often shaped by faculty, university program requirements are often then filtered through university admissions (and community college personnel) before reaching transfer-intending students. Universities exert their power through admissions requirements and through strategic enrollment management decisions, where admissions staff enact the faculty and administration's vision. Four-year institutions often have complex application processes requiring students to complete multiple steps, such as writing application essays, acquiring letters of recommendation, and sending transcripts to the destination institutions, which can be intimidating for students, especially those who have not had to apply to colleges before.[43] Although the process of "transfer" is typically conceived of as a one-time process, many transfer-intending students go through several rounds of applications and decision-making about transfer destinations, resulting in greater application costs, time, effort, and, sometimes, exhaustion with the process overall.[44] Through these processes, particularly the bureaucratic red tape involved in applications, universities send implicit messages about who belongs in higher education.[45] In these ways, the power of four-year institutions—and the policies and practices they enact—substantially shape community college students' transfer trajectories. Thus far, however, the power of universities in shaping the transfer landscape has been largely omitted from scholarship and policy debates.

Shifting the Focus from Community Colleges to the Transfer Field

Although the structuralist perspective highlights how community colleges can create and improve support services for students, it fails to examine institutional transfer from a *field* level, where actors from across multiple organizations, including community college advisors, university admissions personnel, and other staff, interact with each other and with students. In many higher education systems, which historically faced less scrutiny and accountability than K–12 systems, institutions are tenuously linked, with individual colleges emphasizing their own autonomy.[46] Some state policy contexts privilege institutional autonomy more than others, with consequences for transfer pathways and outcomes. Navigating transfer pathways in states with "institution-driven" transfer systems, which give individual institutions more power in shaping transfer requirements, is more challenging for students and advising staff than in states with "2 + 2" systems, where lower-division courses taken at a community college count as the first two years of a degree at state universities. In institution-driven contexts, universities have more control in crafting and filtering policy information.[47]

Transfer processes are complicated by these broader higher education structures. Tensions arise as individual colleges seek their own goals and enact their own procedures for transfer with little regard for other institutions and the needs of students.[48] Both advisors and students are left to navigate the complex information structures that exist because of intersecting and overlapping institutional priorities. Examining that context and how students and staff interact with each other in this landscape can offer greater insights into the challenges community college students face in attaining their educational goals. There is a need to look beyond community colleges to the system level, including public universities and even high schools.[49]

Although scholars and policy makers have highlighted how community colleges, as institutions, can create and improve support services for students, transforming transfer will require moving beyond a singular focus on community colleges. To understand why and under what conditions students successfully transfer, we need to examine the broader environment, including the interorganizational processes and dynamics among community colleges, universities, and state agencies. Processes at both the sending and prospective receiving institutions shape student experiences and outcomes. The role of universities in community college transfer is often overlooked, despite the significant power these institutions hold in shaping transfer processes. By studying institutional transfer at the interorganizational, or field, level, we will further illuminate students' educational pathways, the barriers they face, and how field-level tensions shape their experiences.

Postsecondary Transfer as a Field

Educational institutions are shaped by external pressures and cultural values.[50] In public higher education, the state contexts—and interests of stakeholders—determine the missions of colleges, the programs they offer, the ways they are funded, and our expectations of them.[51] Community colleges are part of complex, loosely coupled higher education systems where institutions operate independently and coordination across fragmented and multilayered institutions is difficult.[52] We leverage an organizational *field* perspective to examine broader interactions across organizations, an approach that moves away from simply examining interactions within organizations—or, in our case, community colleges—to instead focus on the "totality of relevant actors," which can include community college and university personnel and other actors.[53]

In the field of institutional transfer in higher education, actors from multiple organizations, including community college advisors, university admissions personnel, other staff, and students, interact. To facilitate transfer, institutional staff follow agreed-upon rules and procedures for students and support staff. Students must navigate rules and norms to successfully transition from one institution to another, but they are not typically well informed about all the moving pieces in this complex political and institutional landscape. The interactions among community college students, staff, and university personnel are best understood by examining the social order, or field, in which the interactions take place.

Actors, Roles, and Power in the Institutional Transfer Field

We leverage the concept of *strategic action fields*, from organizational theory, to understand the various roles and responsibilities operating within the transfer process. Through this theory, which describes how actors develop and respond to common understandings about the purpose, rules, and relationships in a given social order, we anticipate that institutional actors in different positions react differently to transfer experiences, signals, and events.[54] By focusing on processes that play out as actors work to build and maintain rules and norms in an existing power structure, we can illuminate how political-ecological contexts shape vertical transfer from community colleges to four-year institutions. The theory of strategic action fields foregrounds politics; it focuses our attention on the processes through which actors in the field make choices based on power and their understanding of other actors' roles and of the perceived rules of the field.[55] Strategic action fields serve as a useful tool for understanding how institutional actors from various levels of the higher education system make decisions about credit transfer policies, admissions standards, and the types of transfer information available and for analyzing the actions students take to procure sufficient information to navigate complex and constantly shifting transfer requirements.

Under strategic action fields, we start with four basic tenets: (a) there is generally a shared consensus among actors about what is happening in the field and what is at stake; (b) some actors have more power than others, and actors are aware of their position relative to others; (c) actors operate under a shared set of rules, in which they know which "tactics" are available and appropriate for actors in each role; and (d) actors interpret the moves of others from their own perspective (i.e., they frame those actions based on the other actor's role but also on their own position and role).[56] Unlike previous organizational theories, the theory anticipates that actors in various positions respond differently to events because their relative positions frame their perceptions of opportunities and constraints.

Actors in a field assume several different roles. Our framework delineates between those with dominating influence in the transfer field—those with the most power over transfer rules and norms—and those who hold dominated positions in the field. We outline the role in the transfer field and the positions typically held in the institution in table 1.1.

Dominant actors include *incumbents*, a role typically held by university administrators and faculty, who broadly shape the field due to their power over admissions standards, curricular design, credits transfer, and transfer agreements, and *governance units*, who enforce the rules and norms of the incumbents. The field also includes actors in dominated roles, including positions held by institutional and student actors who are obligated to comply with the rules and often do not question the status quo, a role we refer to as *implementers*. A less common role among dominated actors is that of *challengers*, dominated roles held by actors who seek to push back

Table 1.1. Roles and actions of actors in the community college transfer field

Power	Position/ role	Postsecondary appointment/ affiliation	Goal	Actions taken
	Dominant			
	Incumbents	Administrator or faculty at flagship or other selective university	Preserve integrity of the degree; maintain institution's standards	Block or ignore efforts to create transfer agreements/ guides; resist equating courses across institutions
	Governance units	University admissions representatives, particularly at most selective universities	Preserve selectivity of their institution; maintain rules and norms set by incumbents	Create transfer agreements/guides that adhere to state policy; refer students to posted information or community college agents
	Dominated			
	Challengers	Administrators at community colleges and some less selective universities	Improve clarity of transfer norms/ rules; propose alternatives for institutional and state policies	Create detailed transfer agreements/ guides; conduct outreach to increase communication with multiple actors in field
	Implementers	Community college advisors and students	Adhere to rules/ norms of the field; view following these rules/norms as means to improve transfer success	Provide or collect information about field's rules/norms, depending on position

Notes: The table outlines positions in the field of community college transfer: positions at the top of the table hold the most power in the field and those at the bottom hold the least. We outline the common institutional affiliations of personnel in the different positions. Actors' positions and roles in the field inform their actions in the transfer field.

against the status quo. We next describe each of the roles in greater depth.

Incumbents are actors with "disproportionate influence," whose views are reflected in the priorities of the dominating organization in the field.[57] They define the status quo, where the "purposes of the field are shaped to their interests."[58] In the field of institutional transfer, administrators and faculty at selective, noninclusive universities—particularly flagship universities—serve as incumbents. Incumbents aim to preserve the integrity of their university's degrees and block efforts to equate courses across institutions, usually arguing that their faculty are best suited to deciding which courses should apply toward a given program. Their ultimate goal is to maintain their institution's standards and rank in the field.

Governance units are regulatory units within dominating organizations in the field (as opposed to external government agencies) comprising actors who ensure their "smooth functioning" and "compliance with field rules." Rather than serving as "neutral arbiters of conflicts between incumbents and challengers" (a role sometimes played by government agencies responsible for compliance with legislation), governance units enforce the field's rules, thereby preserving the incumbents' power.[59] Examples of these units include trade associations, accrediting agencies, and departments of internal affairs, which reinforce dominant ideas and safeguard the interests of the incumbents. In the institutional transfer field, university admissions representatives, particularly at the most selective universities, play this role, preserving the selectivity of their institutions by applying rules about admissions in ways that maintain the status quo.

Actors positioned below incumbents and governance units in the hierarchy are dominated actors. They have minimal power, and the actions available to them are dictated by the rules of the incumbents, though some dominated individuals take on the role of challenger. Challengers are aware of the "dominant logic" of the incumbents but envision an alternative social order.[60] They typically comply—albeit reluctantly—with the expectations of their role but also take action toward establishing an alternative field. We conceive of administrators at community colleges and at some less selective universities as challengers who seek to improve the clarity of transfer norms and rules and propose alternative policies that could streamline transfer processes.

Our work also highlights other roles enacted by dominated actors. We provide evidence for a fourth role, *implementers*, who include community college advisors and students.[61] Implementers must adhere to the rules and norms of the field in order to—for advisors—aid transfer, or—for students—meet their goal of transferring. Although roles come with varied advantages, even less powerful actors, such as student implementers, can work to improve their positions.[62] There is a tenuous balance between individuals who have power and "less powerful actors . . . looking to marginally improve their positions."[63]

In this study, strategic action fields help us understand power dynamics among institutional actors and how those dynamics shape interactions among students, transfer staff, and college administrators. In figure 1.1, we offer a new way to conceptualize the field, moving beyond a focus only on community colleges and actors in them. The figure illustrates how transfer-intending community college students are situated

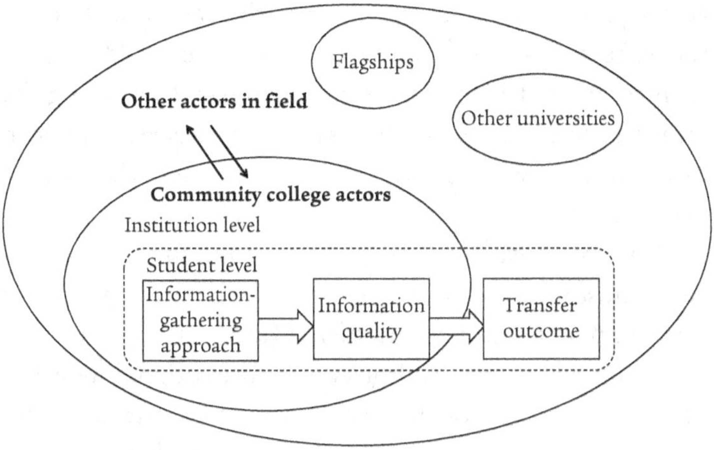

Figure 1.1. Community college transfer field. Figure was adapted from a prior publication in *Sociology of Education*.

within a broader context. University administrators, faculty, and staff wield the most power in the postsecondary transfer field, where universities set standards for admission and credit transfer and selectively share information about those standards. Community college advisors and university personnel maintain information about transfer requirements and admissions standards but don't automatically share it with all students. Both community college and university personnel emphasize students' responsibility for gathering and maintaining their own information about transfer pathways, establishing a shared set of rules where students are held responsible for navigating complex transfer information but sometimes lack the power to access the tools they need.

In addition to considering mesolevel processes that shape transfer—the interactions among individual actors in the field—we also consider microlevel processes among the embedded actors, particularly students, who have the least power but face the biggest consequences. To narrow in on how field-level dynamics shape students' trajectories, in part by shaping the resources, information, and messages they receive for transfer, we examine how students navigate the messages they receive from others.

To make transfer-related decisions, community college students must interpret sometimes competing messages about transfer policies and requirements from varying sources—including community college events, institutional websites, advisors, and policy documents. In the decentralized higher education system in Texas, where institutions have multiple bilateral transfer agreements that determine which courses transfer to which programs, students play a central role in navigating and interpreting policy. Although advisors at community colleges and four-year institutions play roles in shaping how students understand policies, students often "self-advise," curating resources from multiple sources: the web, state agencies, community colleges, and universities.[64] Students from different institutions may receive different signals and different advice. This variation is related partly to policy design: to maintain institutional autonomy, a state may allow different colleges to develop their own core curricula as long as those curricula contain certain broad components.[65] As a result, students receive primarily filtered policy messages from various institutions, with wide variation across the colleges in the composition and quality of the information.[66]

Summary

By developing a field-level perspective on transfer, we move beyond the organizational perspective focused on the community college as a stand-alone institution. We call for a rethinking of transfer students' actions and behaviors, interpreting those behaviors as responses to the field rather than as a function of individual background and interactions with community college staff alone. Our key argument is that community college actors, including administrators, advisors, and students, do not exist in a vacuum. They interact with actors from other institutions in the field, who often have more power. Those interactions shape the "rules of the game," the norms for transfer, and, ultimately, the experiences of community college students who seek to transfer. Rather than place responsibility for transfer outcomes on either the student or the community college actors, we can interpret students' and community college actors' actions in response to a broader set of rules and norms—hidden dynamics that shape the structures of opportunity in higher education. Our study builds on earlier work on this topic, but we focus on field-level rules and constraints to consider the repercussions of the status quo for students and to identify more concrete and impactful ways of improving transfer pathways at the higher education system level.

CHAPTER 2

Privileged Positions Held by University Actors

Standing in front of the iconic tower at the University of Texas at Austin (UT), you can peer down "the six-pack"—a rolling hill flanked by six red-roofed stone buildings—toward the picturesque Littlefield fountain and beyond campus to Texas's sandstone capitol building. Depending on the time of year, you'll find graduates donning burnt orange caps and gowns all along University Avenue, perfecting their photo ops with the tower looming behind them—a symbol of the university and of the state itself. Admissions staff at the university are known to compare students' odds of admission to UT, one of the selective flagship public universities, to those of Harvard. Although those messages are hyperbolic, the state's unusual top 10 percent plan (which, because of enrollment caps, currently guarantees admission to UT for the top 6 percent of graduates from high schools across the state) creates fierce competition for the remaining spots among applicants outside the top of their high school graduating class.

In the past decade, improvements in UT's freshmen retention and four-year graduation rates inevitably resulted in even fewer seats for transfer students, who primarily serve as a backfill for first-time-in-college entrants who leave without completing their degree at oversubscribed selective institutions. In fact, UT's admittance of transfer students has fallen by 30 percent since fall 2011, even as the size of incoming freshmen cohorts increased slightly.[1] Yet UT Austin and Texas A&M University at College Station (A&M)—the other selective flagship university in the state—play outsized roles in transfer policy discussions. These "reach" schools are often the most desired destinations among transfer-intending students, but they also accept far fewer transfer students than other public universities, most of which have strong ties with their local community colleges. Why is it, then, that these elite universities, who are not transfer-receptive, drive transfer policies and pathways in public higher education?

To understand how university personnel shape the transfer pathways and policies of transfer-intending community college students, we interviewed staff from eleven of the most common transfer destinations for our two focal community college districts, Central Community College (CCC) and Fernando Community College System (FCCS). We spoke with personnel from the two flagship universities (the most selective public universities); four emerging research universities (other research-intensive, or R1, institutions striving to increase research productivity and funding); and five regional comprehensive universities (broad-access institutions with minimal admission requirements that draw local students). These interviews offered insights into the power that university personnel have over the transfer landscape. Incumbents—often university administrators and faculty—frequently work to set the standards for admission to certain programs, determine curricula and how credits transfer and apply, and facilitate (or thwart) the development of transfer agreements. Incumbents at the flagship universities hold the greatest power in the field, although those at less prestigious universities benefit similarly from their position in the state's institutional hierarchy, holding more power over credit transfer and program admissions standards than their peers at community colleges.

Guarding Curricular Autonomy: The Role of "Rigor"

Those with incumbent power in the transfer field ultimately act to preserve the status quo: a system that leaves students fumbling through opaque and often misaligned information made available by their community college and desired destination universities. University faculty and administrators produce an environment in which university courses are prioritized as the most rigorous and prestigious, one where students seeking admission to the university jump through hoops to prove themselves worthy but must do so with little support for navigating the system. To university administrators and faculty, their innocuous actions are intended merely to maintain the high standards and rigorous curricula they have come to expect of their programs. Those actions include resisting statewide transfer policy reform, bilateral transfer agreements, and course equivalencies of comparable courses at other public institutions.

Responding to Statewide and Institutional Efforts to Streamline Transfer

In a context that prioritizes institutional autonomy, actors at oversubscribed flagship universities—those with high demand for their limited transfer seats—hold great power in shaping both the implementation of existing statewide policies and conversations about potential reforms. The state's core curriculum was the most prevalent transfer policy described by both staff and students in our study. Texas's core curriculum is a transferable set of lower-division courses, distributed across several component areas. According to state policy, up to forty-two core credits (with credit limits for each of the component subject areas) must be accepted at all public colleges. Students who finish the full forty-two credits across the distributed subject areas are considered "core complete." The core curriculum policy was passed in 1997, with revisions made in 2011 that refined the objectives of the core and the current foundational component areas, such as communications, math, and social/behavioral sciences.[2] Institutions have the autonomy to decide which courses fulfill component areas of the core curriculum, and students can transfer core coursework as a whole or in part—that is, they can transfer "core complete" or with some core credits—but all core credits should transfer to other public colleges.

Unfortunately, although core credits must technically *transfer* between public institutions, there are no guarantees for how those credits will *apply* because of varying degree requirements across institutions. Lower-division core courses may apply differently toward a degree in a given major across different institutions; in some cases, those credits "count," but only as electives, not as major-specific requirements. A student who takes too many—or the wrong—lower-division credits may have excess elective credits at the destination university. Without clarity about how core credits will apply toward a specific program, the core curriculum does not simplify the credit transfer process.

Brian, a director of advising at an emerging research university, explained that institutional autonomy over the core creates a complex web of credit transfer information, putting community college advisors in a tough position:

> I think it's a statewide problem that the community colleges are being asked by their students to not only advise on the community college's requirements but [also on] everybody else's requirements. So it becomes, in reality, very tricky because the advisors at the community colleges, understandably so, may not understand the nuances of core. They say, "Sure, just take any core. It will transfer." Well, yes, *but particular majors do require particular major core courses.* So there is an emphasis [on core], but sometimes that well-meaning emphasis is not necessarily as productive as we would like.

Brian acknowledged that, although a public university must indeed accept core courses, the receiving department sets the requirements of the component majors, and only core courses that align with major requirements will apply toward the program of study; the others will likely count as elective credits. Accruing too many elective credits can ultimately result in wasted time and money for students.

Another policy, Field of Study, addressed some of the challenges of the core curriculum by clarifying how credits apply within specific major pathways for students moving between institutions in the same field. In 2016, as we followed students into their second year of the study, the coordinating board was investing in the state's Field of Study policy. Although the policy had been in place for many years, it had gained little traction at institutions. To build out Field of Study, the coordinating board created committees comprising faculty from community colleges and universities across the state to collaborate in building broad agreements about essential lower-division coursework within specific fields and subfields. Combined, the state's core and Field of Study curricula should have eliminated course duplication for students who switched between public institutions and followed the Field of Study agreements. However, we found that faculty and administrators at the state's universities worked to emphasize institutional autonomy over credit transfer and curricula, minimizing the effectiveness of these state efforts through bureaucratic credit transfer processes and, at times, active resistance to state transfer policies.

Eric, a transfer program coordinator at one of the flagship universities, emphasized that his institution actively discouraged prospective transfer students from transferring into the university with core-complete status. He explained: "I don't believe anyone is telling a student to come in core complete. If anything, there would be a concern that they would get [here], and in particular that first semester, it could be difficult to register for some upper-division courses because you might have the wrong prerequisites. It would be better to have some core curriculum classes in your back pocket that you still need so you can take classes."

By "having core curriculum classes in your back pocket," Eric meant that it is best for students to come to the flagship without having completed their core courses because the university would be unlikely to count core courses from the community college as equivalent to the major-specific core courses required in the destination major. He went on to note that if students did want to come in with their core courses complete, they would need to connect with a UT representative to confirm whether their core courses from the community college would apply toward their desired degree.

Faculty and administrators at state flagships also led efforts to push back against state policies like Field of Study, which they saw as overstepping their institutional autonomy over curricula. Faculty councils at both flagships unanimously voted to oppose the coordinating board's expansion of Field of Study—a policy mandating that approved premajor coursework must apply toward a degree in the same major at any public institution—out of concern that the state was standardizing lower-division coursework. They passed a joint resolution asserting that the "current interpretation of the Field of Study requirements threatens the authority and responsibility of higher education faculty to design curriculum." The faculty council at UT Austin—in the resolution, which was co-signed by A&M's faculty council—delineated their concerns about "unintended consequences related to preparedness, certification, and accreditation." Faculty representatives argued that students completing parallel coursework from other state institutions would be less prepared than students taking their own courses.

The Field of Study policy was not the state's first effort to build statewide collaborative agreements establishing which lower-division courses should be required in degree programs across the state. Tuning Texas, a previous effort, similarly brought together faculty from specific departments and majors to describe their required course sequences and standards in an effort to build transparent statewide transfer guides for that major. Several staff we spoke with described cyclical efforts by the coordinating board to encourage such statewide transfer agreements, including Field of Study and Tuning Texas (through which the collaborative committees created and signed "tuning agreements"). Ben, a director of admissions who oversaw articulation efforts at his regional comprehensive university, said that the state "seems to recycle these [initiatives]" every "ten to fifteen years." He described Field of Study as a reiteration of the same efforts that never seem to change the status quo. (An even newer initiative, the Texas Transfer Framework, was rolled out in 2020.) He elaborated:

> When they started, they brought these universities together across the state, and basically started talking to them and saying, "What do you want to see from community college students that are coming to you?" For example, in engineering: "What do students need to know, and what do these generalized agreements from mechanical, electrical, industrial and maybe chemical engineering need to look like?" It could be called Field of Study now, but when we were first working with them, they were called Texas Tuning agreements.

Ben emphasized that, despite having collaborated to build them, faculty's primary alternate role in the process was ignoring the agreements and returning to the status quo. He explained, "The coordinating board can create new 'tuning agreements' or 'fields of study' et cetera, but ultimately faculty have power over final credit transfer decisions, so *every new initiative results in the same gift wrapped up.*" In other words, university faculty and departments—under current field rules—have the autonomy to ignore these agreements and prioritize their own course sequences. The nonbinding agreements are merely symbolic. After the Tuning agreements were signed (as with Field of Study), the faculty went back to business as usual, admitting students and applying transferred credits based on departmental priorities. The Tuning agreements and Field of Study agreements did not require a transformation of (nor accountability for) internal departmental processes for credit transfer.

Symbolic Bilateral Transfer Agreements

Beyond statewide transfer agreements, the incumbents at flagships thwarted efforts to create meaningful bilateral transfer agreements with partner institutions. The state did not mandate that they create such agreements but instead simply encouraged them to do so. Broader access universities in the state were more likely to respond to pressure from the coordinating board to create transfer agreements across two-year and four-year colleges, but in many cases, university personnel found ways to create generic transfer agreements without sacrificing control over curricula or standards. Kelsey, an administrator at an emerging research university, noted that administrators knew that the symbolic bilateral transfer agreements would "never get to the level where they actually impact students." These "sister-city agreements" were a gesture of goodwill toward community colleges that also cemented current rules and norms. Kelsey added that the agreements suggested only that "we're gonna be nice to you, you're gonna be nice to us. We're gonna obey state laws going back and forth, so . . . we'll honor the core curriculum transferability: we'll accept your students if they meet our admission requirements. But in truth, there isn't a lot of meat beyond what's already expected in those documents. And students never see them. Nor would they understand them if they saw them."

According to Kelsey and several other administrators, going beyond these generic agreements to build program-to-program transfer agreements was difficult because "you had to get into the curricular level," which required faculty incumbents to collaborate. Kelsey explained, "You have to align the curriculum of the two programs." But developing program-to-program agreements can go awry when priorities differ and the two sides are, as Kelsey put it, "not thinking about the same things." The process involved a "swirling around of some emotion and some frustrations," according to Kelsey, because faculty were territorial about their courses and protective of their own interests. Ultimately, Kelsey argued, this dynamic contributed to a transfer field with more generic agreements than program-to-program agreements because university actors "perceive political benefits" of enacting generic agreements. But those symbolic agreements, she said, were "not intended to serve students."

Shaping Programmatic Credit Transfer Information and Processes

Even though admissions personnel often serve as the face—at least to students—of university credit-transfer processes, university faculty and administrators hold the primary power over credit transfer and applicability, whereas admissions personnel implement their preferences and rules. Mike, a student affairs administrator at one of the flagship universities, described decisions about credit transfer and application toward a major as being "delegated to the department heads because the department owns the major." Faculty become "very territorial and very passionate" when deliberating about the acceptance of courses from other institutions (Rick, administrator, FCCS). Unfortunately, that passion is directed toward "quality assurance for the perceived integrity of the degree program" rather than toward ensuring that "students can graduate at the end of it all" (Rick). Harriet, an administrator in enrollment management at a striving research university, described a largely impromptu process by which faculty would determine whether a given course would count at her institution: "If we had a class that had not been transferred in, our faculty or the department chair would review the curriculum in the syllabus to determine if that class was equivalent to a class here. We had some colleges or faculty members that would sit on it for a hundred days, literally, before they would respond." Administrators sought ways to streamline the processes by which departments made credit transfer and applicability decisions. But the faculty had the final say over whether a given course would apply toward the degree program.

Unlike in freshman admissions, university faculty play key roles in transfer admissions, where they determine the standards that must be upheld for admission in a given major. Mike, the director of transition at a flagship university, said:

> The transfer admission here is different from freshman admission. Freshman admission is run entirely by the Office of Admissions. That's not the case with transfer admission

> at our university. The colleges, and in many cases the departments, make the transfer admission decisions. So the transfer application comes in to the Office of Admissions, it's evaluated and processed and so forth, and then it is sent to either the associate dean of the college or, if it's a college that has many departments, those hundreds of decisions may be delegated down to department heads. Decisions are made, in many cases, by the department that *owns the major* the student wants into. The requirements are not standardized . . . some departments are extremely competitive, and the student must know the prerequisite courses and the grade requirements in order to have a better chance of admission.

This expectation that students should do research on admissions standards (e.g., the grades required for a given program), course equivalencies, and credit transfer and applicability is common at many institutions. Mike elaborated, "The biggest barrier to students coming here which they *can* control is (a) knowing the appropriate coursework, and (b) taking the appropriate coursework, and (c) getting the appropriate grade in that coursework. It's mainly coursework. Coursework is the number one thing that these students need to realize is going to dictate their success here. Getting into the university: it's coursework."

But straightforward information about course sequences and credit transfer is typically harder for students to acquire from selective institutions than from less selective, more transfer-receptive institutions. Josh, an administrator who oversees advising at a regional comprehensive university, noted that effective transfer guides need to be specific—rather than a one-size-fits-all-guide—to inform students about the appropriate coursework for their desired program and institution. They also need to be presented in language that students can understand. "I've seen [transfer guides] from the flagships," Josh stated. "They're kind of confusing, actually, because they're very technical, believe it or not. They are not intended for student use. They're intended for academic advisor use or for somebody who actually knows what some of the terminology means."

In the absence of a program-to-program transfer agreement as a basis for a major-specific transfer guide, most transfer guides lead students back to the core curriculum and other statewide policies intended to support transfer. Those transfer guides may be generic compared with a guide that relies on specific pathways mapped out by the receiving institution in partnership with the origin community college. Despite being called "guides," these generic guides do not give students a clear sequence of courses to take to transfer to their major of choice at a particular university. Even when universities do offer program-specific transfer guides, the quality of those guides varies based on how clearly a given department has mapped out its required course sequences, particularly for lower-division courses like those in the core curriculum.

Next, we turn our attention to the role played by admissions personnel, the staff who are tasked with managing and presenting transfer guides and credit transfer information to prospective students. To develop transfer guides and recommendations for applicants, these staff typically draw from the materials available from existing institutional transfer agreements or, when applicable, state policy, as endorsed by incumbents at their institution.

Gatekeeping Through Admissions Criteria and Recommended Course Sequences

University admissions personnel occupy a position of privilege that is slightly different from that of the incumbents, serving primarily as governance units established to enforce the rules and preferences of the incumbents. Although these roles are most influential at selective universities—which hold the most power and set the highest standards for admissions—even admissions representatives at transfer-receptive and less selective universities typically hold more power in the transfer field than community college staff.

Because incumbents at flagship universities prefer not to create bilateral transfer agreements, the universities, as we noted previously, offer major-specific transfer guides that broadly outline the lower-division coursework for each major rather than articulating credit transfer between programs at their institution and specific community colleges. Chris, an admissions administrator at a flagship university, described these documents as "self-guiding tools [intended] to make it simpler for students," while admitting that these guides support the university's goal of providing information without a "guaranteed form of admission." He said it was essential for students to follow transfer guides from the university: "If you are not following what the college has outlined, no, you will not have a smooth transition into admission." Another flagship-university admissions administrator, Kevin, similarly argued that there is "absolutely no way that a student following the guide could take courses that they don't need." But he also acknowledged that this configuration pressures students to decide early on to follow transfer guides from selective universities rather than those of other potential destination universities. If students follow the flagship university's recommended coursework, he stated, those credits "will be good [here], but not for programs not aligned directly with ours." Yet for many students, adhering to only UT's or A&M's transfer guides would be impractical, given low rates of admission at flagships.

By establishing these norms, admissions personnel at the flagships reinforce their institutions' role in the field, signaling that other colleges that want to lower the burden on students could align their curricula with the state's most selective universities. Community colleges that do not conform to those standards heighten the risk that incumbent faculty—who have the final say over credit applicability to the given major—will refuse to recognize students' credits. Transfer-receptive, broad-access universities that do not conform may inadvertently place undue burden on prospective students who may eventually transfer to their institution and lose credits.

Admissions personnel further established and maintained the rules of the field by emphasizing the role that students play as curators of information who must learn and adhere to universities' standards. Kevin, for example, contended that the biggest barriers students face in transferring to a flagship is "failing to plan, and not having the appreciation for the level of rigor that's required here." These sentiments reiterate incumbents' insistence that their university's coursework, sequences, and curricula are more demanding than those of other institutions. Students are unlikely to meet admission standards if they "take a lot of courses that are below the levels normally taught at" the university program, Kevin asserted, making it crucial that departments share their required course sequences so that transfer-intending students can understand how courses from one program will (or won't) be considered equivalent at another institution. Students must both adhere to the recommended courses in their destination program and have strong performance in those courses to combat the "level of competitiveness" of those programs, in which there are sometimes only a few spaces available for continuing students. Flagship universities' enrollment management strategies—accepting transfer students primarily as backfill for first-time-in-college students who did not persist—"put [prospective transfer students] at somewhat of a disadvantage" for accessing the program of their choice (Kevin). Don, an assistant director of admissions at one of the flagships, similarly ascribed responsibility to students for following their transfer guides and course sequences precisely if they hope to be admitted: "I encourage them to look at our [transfer guides] because they'll kind of get a better idea. But if you are not taking the major coursework courses, it's kind of—one of the examples I use—it's kind of hard for a physics department to admit you when you don't have any physics courses completed." With this exaggerated example, he insinuated that many students are unaware of the requirements of their desired degree program and that the materials made available to students are easy to navigate.

In framing transfer problems as attributable primarily to students' lack of preparation, Don resisted the idea that transfer processes are something that could be "fix[ed] at the administration or at the institution or the community college." At the same time, he acknowledged his role as an enforcer of incumbents' tough standards: "I get told sometimes, 'You're being too hard on them and you're being too forward with them,' or 'You're making it sound like we're not able to accommodate.' No! We just may not be the right school for that student that didn't take the initiative to—like I say—trust but verify the information they received. And so we've always tried to empower the student to build that relationship with us."

Here, by noting that students must both *trust* the information they are given by the university and *verify* it, he acknowledged that students might receive information that could lead them astray. As we'll illustrate later on, these dynamics create expectations that students will not just gather but will also curate information from a number of sources and triangulate it across sources to weed out misinformation. This burden is particularly challenging for first-generation college students, who may have fewer trusted individuals to turn to for assistance in navigating transfer information.

Even at less selective universities that serve greater numbers of transfer students, admissions personnel expect students to be able to navigate information about course equivalency and credit transfer on their own, despite evidence—and self-admissions of the personnel—that the posted information is often out of date and riddled with inaccuracies.[3] Casey, a director of undergraduate admissions at a regional comprehensive university, noted that his institution is more likely than others to allow students to apply core credits to their new degree plan; his team in admissions has "leeway to equate courses to the core." They had the authority to decide that a given course fulfills the university's core course requirements, although noncore courses still must be evaluated by faculty within their given major. But he complained that substituting core courses risked "coddling" students and said he preferred that they take the appropriate courses laid out in the university's core curriculum. He placed some blame on community college advisors: "If [students] come in and complain because they were misadvised by their community college, it's not really our fault. We can't always follow the problem by saying, 'Okay, we're going to substitute this course.' Sometimes we don't have that capability. It's just one of those things. Sometimes we have to say no. We can't always bend over backwards to satisfy everybody."

He emphasized the admission department's role in upholding those boundaries and reiterating the standards put forward by faculty in departments, who worked to revise the core curriculum each year.

Information, such as transfer guides and core curricula, is often posted on institutional websites, contributing to admissions personnel's perceptions that students should be able to follow that guidance. Ana Lucia, a transfer admissions recruiter at another regional comprehensive university, explained that, although she thought the information was adequately detailed and easy to follow, most students prefer hands-on help in navigating it: "It's all on the website, but I think the guidance . . . they just want somebody to walk them through it." Unfortunately, at most institutions, students' desire for hands-on support does not align with how transfer-admissions recruitment and advising are set up. Some actors at universities, however, are working to challenge the status quo—by both revising admissions processes and attempting to disrupt underlying preferences of the incumbents—to support transfer students.

Challenging the Status Quo at Universities: Transfer-Receptive Challengers

Occasionally, university student affairs administrators charged with supporting transfer students (primarily at more transfer-receptive universities) bemoaned the "dominant logic" of the incumbents and envisioned an alternative social order.[4] As dominated actors with minimal power in the field, they typically comply, albeit reluctantly, with the expectations of their role, but at times, they also take action toward establishing an alternative field. Chris, an administrator at a striving research university that served a large number of transfer students, acknowledged that even institutions "traditionally seen as transfer friendly may not be living up to that reputation." He described his "institutional goal and personal goal, from thirty-five thousand feet: to regain that reputation of being one of the most transfer friendly institutions you could imagine." But he worried about whether his university could take the steps to "deliver that message." Even at seemingly transfer-receptive universities, the odds can be stacked against transfer-intending community college students. For this reason, the actions available to university challengers are often limited, and changes are small in scale. University-embedded challengers we spoke with primarily work with community colleges to develop transparent information for students and, when possible, advocate for institutional transfer policy changes.

University challengers want transfer-intending students' probability of success to improve, but in service of that aim, these institutional actors usually work to provide additional information to students rather than pushing against the status quo. For example, Margo, a recruiter at a regional comprehensive university, described a problem she identified in her institution's process with determining the "transferability of courses":

> If their transcript says "core complete" and they've met each of their component areas, they're done with their core—but . . . the transcript has to reflect that. There's students that are like, "Oh, I have to take another class, okay, I'll take it." And there's other students like, "Wait a minute, I don't have to take that other class. I've already met it at the community college—why is it not [counting here]?" They question it, and some students don't. You can imagine how many students in the world have taken classes that they don't need because of that.

Margo recognized that her university did not always give students credit for core courses unless their transcripts said "core complete," despite the state policy stating that each core course must transfer even if a student is not core complete. To counter what she perceives as unfair practices of credit transfer, she urges students to have their transcripts marked to avoid having to take additional posttransfer core courses. Although well intentioned, this approach ultimately puts burden back on students to ensure that the university complies with the policy and that credits transfer as dictated by that policy.

Another university challenger at a regional comprehensive university—Josh, the director of advising initiatives, who had complained about flagship universities' overly technical transfer guides—works to combat the status quo of murky transfer guidance. When he began his role, prospective students had to "use our transfer equivalency guide, which is online, through our admissions office." Through the web tool, students could use "this giant kind of search function" to either individually examine "every course that has been evaluated and articulated from all the institutions we've been accepting courses from," or, if they selected their community college, "it [would give] you this huge, long document that we tell them flat out not to print because it's going to be like ninety pages with course-to-course crosswalks." The course-by-course search function and the community college–specific document put a lot of burden on students to navigate course equivalencies. The process spurred Josh to create simple and accessible transfer guides, drawing from his institution's program-to-program transfer agreements and using language that makes sense to students: "We want something they can read and understand too." He also emphasized the need for his institution to "be a lot more aware that, as a campus, most of our population is transfer students, and as a culture [we need] to understand what they're coming from." To further support students' navigation of the transfer process, he developed a "pre-transfer advising program where the advisors go out to the campuses of our four largest transfer partners and talk to the students about what they need to do to transfer and how [the advisor] can help out that process and facilitate things." This strategy enables students to get direct guidance from the prospective institution, meaning they can ask questions and troubleshoot when they find information and standards to be unclear.

Transfer personnel and student affairs administrators who oversee transfer programming at transfer-receptive universities often described creating new structures to improve the transparency of admissions standards and credit transfer processes. Brian, a transfer coordinator at a striving research university, rationalized that most students "really don't know where to transfer." When considering their options, he said, students find that "everybody has different rules, different policies, and we're different schools," making it even harder for students to compare them. He continued, "You can't fault us all for doing it differently, but I think there has to be a little more ownership on the part of universities that are accepting students from these public institutions than 'Let's make this as seamless as possible.'" Of course, the incentive to develop a more seamless process is stronger at universities for which transfer students are—as one administrator from a regional comprehensive university put it—the "lifeblood of [their] institution." Unlike at flagship universities or even at striving research universities, regional comprehensive universities often have historical ties to their local community colleges, relying on them to meet their enrollment goals. In that way, university personnel at broader access universities serve as captive collaborators who are eager to meet the needs of transfer-intending community college students, but they also lack the power and privilege of incumbents at the most selective universities to push for larger scale changes in the state.

Although most university challengers occupy student affairs positions at transfer-receptive universities, we found some instances in which student affairs personnel at the flagships worked to make small inroads toward change, primarily through efforts to shift long-held beliefs of faculty and administrators about transfer populations. Stella, a transfer program coordinator at one of the flagships, reported: "I still talk to faculty who believe these myths about transfer students: that they were not good enough to get in, and are a drain. [But] their grade point average is [the same], if not higher, than [that of] freshmen." In her work supporting transfer programing, she strives to inform faculty about the level of preparation of transfer students and their strong performance in university coursework. Within their institutions, these flagship-based challengers are more inclined to connect with personnel from community colleges to collaborate on improving transfer transparency for students than their incumbent and governance-unit peers.

Summary

In this chapter, we illustrate that university actors, as incumbents and governance units, hold substantial power in the transfer field. The dominant players we talked with at the state's public universities work to emphasize institutional autonomy, pushing back against statewide transfer policies. Their efforts, including their tight control of credit transfer, preference for opaque credit-transfer information, and resistance to state transfer policies, stymie the effectiveness of existing policies and precluded reforms and cross-sector collaboration. University faculty and administrators—and admissions representatives, acting on their behalf—determine how courses count toward a bachelor's degree; their curricular influence trickles down throughout the state. By setting the rules and norms of the transfer field to emphasize their own priorities, university actors ultimately shape a field that does not seek to facilitate transfer but, rather, to maintain the standards set by universities. As we'll explore in chapter 3, community college staff are typically dominated actors tasked with enacting field rules (implementers), although some question dominant practices and norms while reluctantly reinforcing the status quo (challengers).

CHAPTER 3

Implementers and Challengers in the Community College System

On the northern outskirts of a city in Texas, nestled between a quiet neighborhood of cul-de-sacs, newer tract homes, condos, and a busy two-lane divided roadway, sits the four-building campus of one of the local community college districts. The four buildings surround a central quad. The campus, which has been in operation for over twenty-five years, was mostly empty midmorning on the Friday we arrived. The sun was beating down with September heat. We were there to observe a transfer event that was to bring community college students into direct contact with representatives from universities in an effort to help the students navigate the transfer process. At the event, a community college staff member gave general advice to approximately fifteen students about applying to transfer to universities. Then she introduced a panel of eight representatives from public and private universities in the state before encouraging students to consider "at least five universities," advice echoed by a panelist who suggested that students should broaden their search because "life happens." The panel offered a key opportunity for transfer-intending students to learn from university representatives—to ask questions, learn about tuition rates, and get a sense of campus life at each of the universities. After the panel, students were told they could approach representatives individually with specific questions.

In the Texas transfer context, it was necessary for community colleges to facilitate this type of direct connection with university representatives to provide students with information about their options and because, as we described in chapter 2, universities hold substantial power over transfer processes. Universities can change programmatic requirements on a whim and have a significant amount of discretion about how to implement state transfer policies. Students thus need to be in regular communication with university representatives to know what courses will and will not apply toward their program of choice. One of the panelists at the transfer event we observed, for example, described how, at his flagship university, students need two additional lower-division courses, beyond the completion requirement at the community college, to be admitted. Therefore, even if a student completed all the basic requirements for their associate degree, that would not be sufficient for the student to be admitted as a transfer student to the program of their choice at this flagship university. Camila, an advising leader at the community college, explained why this type of constant pretransfer communication with universities was so important: "That's my main thing, is access to the universities. So what I've really done in the last year is built up access. I've asked universities to come out, to sit down with the students here. It's been done off and on before, but what I've pushed is for them to be here on a more consistent basis." Given that community college staff lack reliable information about transfer (and the power to shift transfer requirements and standards), such transfer events are critical for connecting students to the most powerful actors in the field, who also have the most up-to-date information.

Despite hosting these types of events, community college staff noted the continued challenges of advising students in such a decentralized system, where their role was shaped by informational and power asymmetries. During one of our site visits, we met with Lloyd, a community college professor who also advised students. We observed him in his office as he met with students individually to discuss their transfer plans. He explained that each university had its own requirements for which math courses would transfer and that these requirements varied within universities, by college. For example, there could be different requirements for the College of Liberal Arts or for engineering schools within a university. Even when students transferred as "core complete"—having fulfilled all forty-two credit hours required in the core curriculum, spread across the various component areas—they would often arrive at the university and be told they needed to take more classes. Lloyd asked, "Who is going to advocate for the students?" and described how, in his experience, students often had to "argue" with the transfer institution and "insist on" the courses transferring to obtain credit. Not all students were aware of this or prepared to petition in this way for their courses to count toward their degrees—many simply lost credits.

Nina, a transfer administrator at a community college, similarly noted: "The articulation agreements that we have with our two largest transfer partners, they are what I would call generic. Literally, they're labeled 'general articulation agreements.'" She explained that the agreement says that, for any degree program that the community college offers that has a corresponding degree program at the university, the university will count those courses toward the bachelor's degree requirements. She added, "However, on the ground, we know that doesn't happen in that implied seamless manner, because a student will, for example, get to [the university] and say 'Well, I'm core complete.' . . . They accept the course—it does count—but it doesn't satisfy that specific degree requirement." This situation would lead to the student's having to take another core class to satisfy the requirement for their major, resulting in extra credits and costs for the student. Nina concluded, "Unfortunately, we have way too many circumstances where we know our students encounter that in the transfer process."

Because of the different incentives and the disproportionate power held by universities, especially flagships, students were often told by universities that they should transfer at thirty credits, but students could save money if they transferred at sixty credits, remaining enrolled in less-expensive community colleges for a longer period before transferring. Switching to a university early could prevent some of the challenges of transferring courses, but for a higher price tag, and students were not always fully aware of their options. Lloyd noted that there was "no consistency" and said he believed there should be a "state-mandated way" of transferring credits so that students did not have to receive and navigate conflicting information from their community college and transfer destination. Despite his passion and commitment to his students, there was little that Lloyd, as a dominated actor in the community college system, could do, other than teach his students to advocate for themselves on a case-by-case basis.

Exploring the Role of Challengers and Implementers in Community Colleges

As we described in the previous chapter, university actors, particularly at flagship universities, dominate the transfer landscape—they seek to preserve the status quo, which they argue maintains the integrity of their standards and of a bachelor's degree from their institution. Therefore, they resist—often successfully—efforts to streamline course transfer between community colleges and four-year institutions. In contrast, community college actors hold dominated positions. They seek to effect change where they can, but there is little they can do *within* the scope of their institutions to drive the types of policy reforms needed to truly alter the transfer process *between* institutions.

Previous research on strategic action fields acknowledges that some dominated actors—*challengers*, like Lloyd and Nina—envision an alternative to the social order and either begrudgingly enact their role in the field or take steps to change the social order;[1] yet there has been little focus on variation among dominated roles. In the transfer field, we found that the most prevalent dominated role is one we call *implementers*; this position is held by institutional and student actors who are obligated to abide by the rules and often fail to question the status quo. Although they share similar goals, institutional implementers have more power than student implementers. In this chapter, we shift to explore the nondominant roles in the transfer ecology.

Focal Institutions: Central Community College and Fernando Community College System

Over the course of our six years of interviews with transfer-intending community college students, we also interviewed administrators and transfer services personnel at their colleges, Central Community College (CCC) and Fernando Community College System (FCCS) (see the appendix for additional information on the institutional contexts). We asked about institutional policies and practices and about staff perspectives on the transfer process. From these interviews, we learned about the ways that challengers and implementers engage with other actors in the transfer field. Next we describe the goals of and actions available to community college challengers and staff implementers.

Frustrated by the Status Quo: Challengers Within the Community College System

In the previous chapter, we described how some actors at transfer-receptive four-year institutions seek to challenge the status quo and improve transfer dynamics, despite reluctance on the part of flagship and selective institutions of higher education. Similarly, we found that some community college personnel voiced frustration about the fact that the field disadvantages transfer-intending community college students and envisioned ways to improve the transfer process. Community college–based challengers were most often community college administrators with concerns over problems students faced in transferring credits and navigating misaligned degree requirements across universities.

Challengers sought to clarify transfer requirements and standards by developing partnerships and collaborating with universities, and, at times, they proposed alternatives to institutional and state policies. They often worked to create detailed transfer agreements and guides and to connect multiple actors in the field. Community college challengers in our sample built a regional collaborative partnership across public institutions to develop transfer agreements, requesting that partner universities publicly post information for students and adhere to the state's common course-numbering system. Such changes, they argued, would make it easier for students to understand lower-division course alignment across institutions.

One transfer staff member at CCC, Alicia, an advisor, described how she maintained partnerships with other schools to ensure her students got the information they needed. She convened meetings between staff from universities and community college staff to talk about program changes. Through these meetings, she met with several large public universities in the area. Alicia told us: "We talk with them, they come in. They give us information. Because our articulation and transfer department works with the universities, and they set up the days where we can meet with individual institutions.... We can get that information from that university to bring it back and discuss it with our students: 'This is a very competitive program. You got to have a certain GPA to get into it.' So it helps." Much of this work occurred behind the scenes, working to bring faculty and administrators together to manage articulation agreements and one-to-one events between community colleges and four-year institutions.

Some of these administrators built a regional collaborative partnership across public institutions to develop transfer agreements. Val, vice president of student services at Central Community College, believed the partnership "held a lot of promise to build aligned curricula" and reduce credit loss. However, she noted that university administrators opposed a common course-numbering system, saying, "I don't know if the will is there" and "It's going to take legislative action." Val added, "This is as close as we've gotten to a more broad collaboration with our prospective partners." In their efforts toward the regional partnership, these administrators worked with the universities, at both the administration and the department levels, to build institution-wide buy-in from the universities. However, Val noted that "this has always been one of the big challenges with regards to trying to get this statewide, or even university-to-college, collaboration."

The onus is often on the community college to foster these relationships, to be more proactive and less reactionary in meeting students' needs. Sofia, a transfer services director at one community college, described how she worked with faculty at local universities to "align" their programs. She noted that a key part of her role was to help university faculty understand that there were "things hindering a student's successful transfer" because coursework was "misaligned." Here, too, however, the work fell to community college staff to broker relationships with four-year institutions.

The regional collaborative also sought to develop technology to allow students to track their progress through transfer. Its members aimed to use these data to inform further transfer supports. The community college partners were "very intentionally" creating "degree plans that are indeed aligned" with those of the common destination universities, to the extent possible. Val added that the work included "bringing two-year and four-year faculty together at the program level to build curricul[a]." She observed, "I think it's an attempt to try and get some regional collaboration, broad university collaboration. The president [of each institution] will need to be signing on this agreement, and the presidents and counselors helping to facilitate this kind of work. We're still in the midst of finalizing that. The work still hasn't begun yet. I think it holds a lot of promise."

Unfortunately, despite this promise, some universities in the area stymie progress toward a regional transfer agreement that would address the aims laid out in the original vision, primarily taking issue with what they perceive as the standardizing of lower-division coursework through requiring common course numbers. As Nina noted: "The fact that we have five different university systems in our state and the politics that go with those—that's just the way it goes. We've gotta try to work with that, and with that other capital P, which is the politics and the power struggles that go on between the players in these different university systems. I don't think that can be overestimated. That's just the nature of higher ed in Texas." Here, Nina spoke directly to the power dynamics we described in the previous chapter, where some actors in the higher education system have power and dominance and thus shape the field of transfer for all.

Ultimately, these inefficiencies and barriers between institutions make it harder for students to transfer. The lack of consistency and communication between institutions make it, according to Celeste, a community college advising leader, "a little more difficult for the community college students," especially first-generation college students. In response to a question about what barriers community college students face with transfer, she placed the bulk of the responsibility on four-year institutions. She noted that universities will say that community college students "aren't prepared for their expectations," but she believed that "four-year universities are actually making it more difficult for our students" by "continuously evolving . . . the classes and courses and core requirements." She described sitting in meetings where "the professionals at the four-years are saying, 'Well, we're not taking *a* and *b* [courses]. We're not taking [those]—we prefer them to take this here. We prefer they take this there.'"

University preferences—which frequently change over time—shape students' experiences during the transfer process. In contrast to this current system of misalignment, Celeste described a vision for altering the field: "I would like to see a meeting of the minds that there are seamless pathways created for students from the first hour to the 126th hour or 130th hour. I would like us all to be responsible and accountable to the students and not to the institution." Celeste described how the regional collaborative sought to work toward this goal, challenging the status quo, but noted that the most powerful actors were not on board. She said: "I think the conversations are happening, but the people at the table are not the ones to make the changes. So I can sit all day with the likes of you and the likes of my peers that all expressed this, but we are not the agents of change." Indeed, at the regional collaborative meetings we attended, we noted limited engagement from the flagship institutions, but we did see larger turnout among regional comprehensive four-year institutions, particularly those with personnel we characterized as "challengers" to the status quo.

Although the community college administrators have held meetings for the collaborative, several universities refused to sign the agreement or participate because the collaborative required partners to use the common course-numbering system. Indeed, common course numbering was mentioned as the "biggest issue" faced by students that cannot be resolved solely through the community college system, according to Nina at CCC. She said of the common course-numbering system:

> We need it. We really do. Everybody just needs to get on board with it, because it is very confusing to figure out which university takes which one of our [specific classes] and which university will take [another] . . . if they want a certain sequence. We have great transfer guides, but it would make the university's job easier and our job easier if we all just agreed that English is English 1301 everywhere and not English 16K or whatever. Those types of things. That would be the biggest help to make it less confusing.

However, a common course-numbering system is an issue that requires collective agreement across institutions, and some universities are not willing to adopt it, arguing it would standardize lower-division coursework. Without coordination across institutions, students and advisors have to compare courses at their community college with each individual potential transfer destination to work out which courses will count toward a given degree.

These community college staff members are *challengers,* working, often with limited success, to transform the status quo in hopes of easing transfer and university access for students. Yet most staff are *implementers,* who largely accept the field as it is and believe it is primarily the students' role to inform themselves. These staff members are knowledgeable about the transfer field but cannot keep up with the rapid changes and varying requirements across programs; thus, most of the work of navigating specific transfer pathways falls on students.

Implementers in the Community College System

In contrast to challengers in the community college system, staff implementers argue that adhering to the existing rules and norms (rather than trying to transform them) is a means to improving transfer success. One advisor explained that the "advisor's job" is to "remind and promote information about transfer opportunities" and to "organize and present all of the universities' requirements." Therefore, implementers provide information about existing transfer policies and practices to students. Ultimately, though, we found that community college staff maintain the social order by continuing to implement and reinforce the rules and norms set by universities, particularly through their high expectations for students to gather and triangulate information.

The staff who work most closely with transfer-intending community college students—often general community college advisors or transfer-specific advisors—frequently serve as cogs in the system, managing the vast array of university program requirements and information. Camila, an FCCS advisor, explained: "We're working on a list of all of the universities' requirements. . . . The deadline, the financial aid FAFSA code, their application requirements . . . their minimum credits. Their maximum credits of transfer." One community college advisor at CCC explained that advising is "very prescriptive in outlook . . . really, it's the transfer guide that's determining what students must take." In other words, the advisors primarily work to translate information in the guides for students seeking to transfer.

Another CCC advisor, Mark, similarly explained that most information is posted online, where the advisor's role is to help students access that information:

> As far as a central place students can look at, it would be our transfer website. . . . They try to put a bunch of information there. There's information for different universities, generally the ones we send a lot of students to. Students can generally access transfer guides from universities that provide those to us. Just to kind of limit the questions. "What class do I need for this particular major at the university?" It's all right here, and if you follow that, there's not gonna be any surprises.

Mark noted that if students follow these guides, there won't be "any surprises," but, as we learned from other advisors, and from students, that was not always the case. Surprises did occur once students transferred and learned that some courses would not count toward their majors. At the same time, Mark described how he tried to fill in any gaps in students' information. If there were questions he couldn't answer, he would call around to universities to try to get answers, deeming it his responsibility to figure it out for students.

Although Mark has built a personal network of university staff whom he can call at particular institutions, the communication is not always smooth. He described how he and other advisors at the community college work to get the information they need from university officials:

> Everyone that's involved in transfer [services] meets generally once a month, to make sure all of the information's up to date. We try and get to a central location and kinda go from there. Communication's pretty good for the most part. I think if there was anything that would probably help, I think it would be coming from the universities specifically. "Hey, this has changed for transfer students. This is what we're doing now, as opposed to what we did in the past." Any updates like that coming from the universities would definitely be helpful.

Advisors, he said, are expected to "maintain knowledge about what the policies are, and what students need to get to a particular school." This often requires having some sort of system to manage material from various universities, some with hundreds of programs. From there, he noted, there are strategies to "navigate around some of these issues," and he mentioned that it "sometimes becomes a bit of a game, to try and figure out how we can make something happen" to get more accurate information for students. He believed that advisors at the community college were doing their part with the information they had but that "getting the information from the universities is priority number one." The process of disseminating information from the universities to students is complex, as the information "goes from the university to our articulation people, our transfer people, and then from there it gets disseminated out," but Mark felt they did "a pretty decent job" of sharing the information they have with students. He expressed that the real challenge and place for improvement was "getting the information from particular universities so that we're up to date" on the specific credit transfer requirements for each university.

Relying so much on university partners for up-to-date information on their credit-transfer policies makes advising challenging in community college systems. Given the array of requirements and variation in programs, advisors acknowledged that they cannot always keep up with this task. Nina lamented the difficulty of transfer advising: "Advisors are expected to know everything about every [university], and really that's impossible. With things changing all the time, with catalogs changing, policies changing, it's really impossible to know everything." She added: "One of the things that we find to be challenging and that would help students is right now the advisors and counselor here at CCC, we do advising for CCC, but we also need to know every university and every college, as well. So I think having more university representation on our campuses would help the students, because they could get the information direct from the source." She described community college staff as knowledgeable but noted that the expectations are too high. She added: "I would say they're [students are] pretty lucky here at CCC because all of our advisors are versed in transfer. So I would say our advisors are very prepared."

Ana Lucia, a university staff member who was based at a community college, distinguished her responsibilities from those of her university colleagues. She provides information to students, but her university colleagues have the power to make decisions about how credits transfer. Ana Lucia said that, when working with students, "I'll give them a general analysis of their university transcript. We use our equivalency table on our website, on our university admissions website . . . so we can give them a pretty good idea [of] what's going to transfer." However, she noted that there are limitations:

> We're not going to be able to tell them how their courses are going to transfer, especially if—say for instance they took an education class or a business class and there's not a direct equivalent of that course but it does transfer, the department within their major would have to determine if that course is acceptable. That requires an appeal and all that good stuff once they're a student here, once they're admitted. We don't make those decisions that the dean or the chair makes or the advisor makes. What we're doing is we're just trying to give them a general idea on "Yes, the courses will transfer because it's from an accredited institution," but *how the course is going to apply* to your degree plan has to be ultimately decided by the department or the advisor.

As Ana Lucia's words illustrate, departmental advisors, department chairs, and deans at the university have the final say on how credits apply toward a degree plan, which Ana Lucia clearly distinguished from those credits transferring. Although credits may technically transfer, they can end up counting as generic electives if the receiving department does not agree that the credits fulfill major requirements of the program's degree plan. As described in chapter 2, university faculty have a great deal of power over credit transfer and application; the student-facing staff at community colleges work to learn and inform students of those rules.

A System That Shifts the Burden of Transfer to Students

Community college staff and advisors work to collate information from a variety of sources and consider it their role to guide students. Yet many advisors also place the responsibility for seeking information about transfer and pursuing additional transfer guidance on students. Staff acknowledge that if students do not ask about transfer directly, they will not receive information; advisors typically share transfer resources with students upon request. Advisors told anecdotes about students who accumulated credits that may not count toward transfer because they had been engaging in "self-guidance" (i.e., not regularly seeing an advisor). Celeste, an advisor at FCCS, explained that "a lot of [students] come in" and "they have not educated themselves," adding that students are often unaware of the various transfer options and how to evaluate them. Sofia, a transfer director at CCC, noted that students need to be "self-directed" and take "ownership of what they are doing." This stance stems directly from how she sees the role of the transfer team: as being there to provide "support" and "encouragement" while helping students make "well-researched, sound decisions." Sofia sees a successful student as one who "utilizes the resources [the institution] offer[s]" and who "participates" in the programs. Sofia attributes students' successful transfer, when it occurs, to this labor-intensive resource gathering: "they're successful because they've done the work." She does not question whether the workload of comparing and fact-checking across various transfer information sources should, in fact, be less of a challenge for students. When asked what would make a student unsuccessful, she replied: "A lack of planning early. A failure to ask questions. We encourage students to talk to everybody, connect with the universities, ask the universities, ask us, ask your professor, ask everyone, ask every question." Here, again, advisors expect students to connect with multiple stakeholders to gather information; the time intensity of this task, especially for students who have external obligations, is typically overlooked or even thought of as the simple cost of transfer success.

Although many advisors acknowledge the complexity of the transfer landscape, including varying transfer pathways (hundreds of combinations of universities and majors) and holes in publicly posted transfer information (including a lack of transfer guides in many majors), several believe that students are not taking advantage of available information. Students' responsibilities are to be ahead of the game when it comes to gathering transfer information. Camila, a transfer director at FCCS, noted that she expects students to get information early from prospective four-year universities. She also said that students "do not see the importance of getting information early," which presents challenges for staff. She shared that staff at FCCS "never ever" suggest destination universities to students because they "want the student to make the decision." This practice may avoid allegations that students are being steered toward particular universities, but it also puts more responsibility on students to assess which schools might be a good fit for them. She said she expected students to "research, research, research" to identify appropriate programs, examining "the tuition, the program, how many transfer credits they allow."

Because they acknowledge that publicly posted transfer information is often flawed, community college advisors like Camila encourage students to meet with university representatives who "have the most knowledge." At the same time, institutional implementers described students struggling to connect with university staff. Some universities have norms of "not advising non-students," as Tim from CCC noted, and these university staff send all inquiries back to general admissions recruiters, who often cannot tell students how or whether credits will count toward a given degree. Another CCC advisor, Dennis, felt like the community college staff were making progress in changing these systems. In the past, a community college student could receive advising from the local flagship universities only after they had been admitted as a student, but Dennis said: "They could talk to the undergraduate program where the undeclared students would go . . . but, in the specific area, they couldn't talk to someone." In this previous arrangement, students were unable to access the information they needed to learn how their courses would apply to their major. However, Dennis noted that this policy was changing because of a shift in the "atmosphere and climate" between the community colleges and four-year institutions as both parties seek to smooth the transfer processes between institutions.

Community college actors work within a broader structure, where universities hold the most power. There is only so much that they can do, yet they often take the blame for sharing misinformation about transfer requirements, even though many policies are beyond their control and they are not directly responsible for many of the sources of transfer information. Andrea, an FCCS transfer advising lead, noted that changes from the university staff are sometimes communicated slowly, which results in students' being misinformed. "Sometimes we run into situations. . . . Sometimes they—like the colleges won't approve things in time, like for the catalogue, or if there's a new class that they've created that's changed. We had an agreement that a class was gonna transfer, yet we don't always get word right away that they've changed the curriculum. We're here telling students: 'Yes, that class is gonna transfer.' They get there and it doesn't. That's just—that's bad." She explained that "for the most part," the agreements with four-year institutions are "pretty seamless" but acknowledged that they face occasional "hiccups" with the agreements. She elaborated, saying: "It's not good because that student just spent all this money and time, but a class is not gonna transfer." In cases where they cannot give a "100 percent guarantee" on whether a class will transfer, she said, she directs students to the universities: "I can't guarantee this, but here's how you can reach out to [University A or University B], or wherever."

This system of referring students back to the source of the information, however, can also lead to a "blame game" of sorts. One director of transfer services at CCC noted that there were media articles highlighting how students spent thousands of dollars on "wasted classes," and the media attention prompted a blame game in which the students point at community college advisors as the source of bad advice, the advisors point at the student for not making their transfer intentions clear or at the university for not aligning their programs, and the university blames the community college for providing inaccurate information. We argue that the real blame, however, must be placed on the *system* or transfer *field*, which is so decentralized and uncoordinated (with sending and receiving institutions operating with little accountability) that it allows for out-of-date information or misinformation to be spread without sufficient checks, creating confusion for actors involved. The consequences of this system, and the power dynamics between community colleges and universities, are ultimately felt by transferring-intending students who are forced to negotiate these complex webs of information in pursuit of their educational aspirations. In chapter 4, we focus on the experiences of students navigating transfer and on how the dynamics between institutional actors in the transfer field shape student outcomes.

CHAPTER 4

Students as Implementers

We now return to the case of Teresa, a Texas-born Latina who was the first in her family to attend college. We met Teresa during her second semester of community college and followed up with her five times over the next six years. During these conversations, we learned about how she navigated the transfer process. She expressed several times that she did not really know a lot about transferring and had not received sufficient information. Even in her third year at the community college, she remained confused about whether to obtain an associate degree before transferring and about how that coursework would align with coursework at her transfer destination. By year four, she had decided not to pursue the associate degree because she was still unsure of whether and how the credits would transfer. Even though Teresa turned to advisors for answers and for assistance with course selection, she felt confused about the transfer process. She knew that her "basics," or her core courses, should transfer, but she was not sure about how many of them would, or how they would apply to her specific major. Many students, like Teresa, remained *misinformed* or *underinformed* about the transfer process; they were missing key information that would help them determine which courses to take at the community college given their intention to transfer, which destination programs and institutions aligned with their needs and goals, and when in their college career to transfer.

Students used various strategies to collect the transfer information they needed, often *curating resources* from multiple sources. Teresa, for example, sought resources beyond her advisors, using an online degree-planning tool that her community college provided and Google searches to find additional information online. But despite these efforts, she remained uneasy about credit transfer. When it came to selecting "core classes I can take here that will apply over there," she noted, "it's not really easy to google it." In the decentralized transfer environment of Texas, she said, she realized that "every case is different." Given the lack of broader coordination across institutions, the information she found online sometimes conflicted with what advisors told her, and sometimes counselors and other advising staff could not help her with her specific questions.

To find relevant transfer information, Teresa curated from several different resources (i.e., websites, guides, and staff members). As she explained in her third year at the community college, "Most of the universities will have a specific transfer tab in there and so you can just look in there. . . . It usually has what I need. If it doesn't have what I need, then I go to a counselor and they help me find it." She had to triangulate information across sources because she noticed that "the counselors, the teachers, and the financial aid people are always, like, butting heads." That was the case, she noted, "because the teachers [are] like, 'Oh no, don't do that.' And the financial aid people are like, 'Don't do that, that's going to mess with your financial aid'; but the counselors aren't really looking at that, they're looking at, like, what's good for you or your classes or whatever." Although she sought to obtain as much information as she could on transfer pathways and how to maximize her credits from the community college, when Teresa transferred in her fourth year to a regional university, she still lost several credits and expressed frustration about having wasted time and money on courses that would not apply toward her degree.

Students as Implementers: Gathering Information on Transfer

As we noted in previous chapters, staff expected that students would connect with personnel at their community college and prospective transfer destination when planning for transfer. Teresa, however, interacted with someone at the university only *after* she had transferred. Similar to community college actors who enacted and disseminated information about transfer rules, transfer-intending community college students operated as *implementers* in the transfer field. Their role involved gathering information about the field's rules to improve their probability of success, though student implementers had the least power of all actors in the transfer field. Critical components of the broader ecological contexts—the relationships between incumbents, challengers, and community college implementers—shaped how transfer-intending students experienced the transfer process. In this chapter, we illuminate how a field-level approach to understanding transfer offers new insights about the experiences of transfer-intending students.

Staff and students agreed that students bear the primary responsibility for gathering information about transfer requirements. One student, Maya, described the tension between doing her own research and taking advice from community college staff: "I met with the counselor [in] early summer, but she didn't really tell me anything that I didn't find out on my own. I obsess. I will print the things, and put them next to each other, and kind of check-mark them. I need to see the progress. All they do is go on and look at the same screen I was looking at. I asked questions to make sure: 'Are you sure this is the class, not this?'" Maya saw her role in the field as one in which she had to continuously fact-check information to improve her chances of transferring. She relied primarily on her research, checking with her advisor for additional verification.

For students, implementing the rules of the transfer field required gathering information that can be difficult to find or interpret. We observed variation in how students enacted their role: some were more likely to seek out information from various sources, and others leaned more heavily on one or two sources. Their different approaches appeared to have consequences for transfer outcomes. Students varied in whether they were able to build adequate information to move toward their transfer goals. We identified three "tracks" that represented the quality of students' transfer information at the time of the second interview: *sufficiently informed*, *informed but misguided*, and *underinformed*. Students who appeared to be sufficiently informed described having access to relevant transfer information that aligned with their goals, were aware of the options available to fulfill those goals, and identified actionable information without glaring inconsistencies or misinformation. Students who were informed but misguided also described transfer information they had collected, but the information included clear inconsistencies or inaccuracies that they either had not noticed or had not resolved. Finally, students who were underinformed lacked sufficient information to achieve transfer goals; they did not describe having a transfer guide or reported that they had no information related to transferring into a desired major program or university. Over half—56 percent—of students in our sample were sufficiently informed, 34 percent were informed but misaligned, and the remaining 10 percent lacked sufficient transfer information. Their information-gathering approach—and the resulting quality of their transfer information—shaped their transfer outcomes.

Information-Gathering Approaches

We identified four themes that describe students' responses to their role as implementers through their information-gathering approaches. Several students *curated resources*, collecting transfer information from a variety of sources and comparing, contrasting, and synthesizing to identify trustworthy insights. *Hesitant advisees* similarly worked to find their own information about transfer procedures and requirements but typically eschewed advisors, often as a result of negative prior experiences. *System trusters*, on the other hand, put their faith in advising staff to lead them through the rules and requirements for transfer, often relying on them entirely for navigating the transfer process. *Disconnected students* did not seek additional information to move toward their transfer aspirations or clarify their transfer plans, which often left them disconnected from essential transfer resources and services, even at their own institution. In this section, we illustrate how students' information-gathering approaches shaped their transfer experience, whether they had sufficient information for navigating complex transfer pathways, and whether they transferred.

Resource Curators

Resource curation—by which students sought and "triangulated" information about transfer from a variety of sources—was the most common approach across our sample (used by about 60 percent of students). After gathering information from various sources, including community college staff and faculty, university admissions staff, friends and family, and institutional websites, resource curators worked to synthesize information.

These students described the need to "be strategic" about vetting transfer information and identifying which items they deemed most trustworthy, often in response to receiving misinformation from advising staff. Sam, a first-generation college student intent on earning a bachelor's degree in engineering, described his experiences with advising staff at CCC:

> The counselors here are really hit or miss. The first counselor I talked to, I was like, "And this is what I want to do. I want to go to [this university]. I want to transfer into electrical engineering." She just set me up: "Here is our general engineering plan." So she had me in chemistry and stuff like that. Then I was wondering about it, so I started researching

> the university's website. I found their transfer process. They have a PDF of everything they want you to take, and a lot of her advice wasn't on that. So I was going to waste time taking classes I don't need.

After realizing that different engineering majors have different requirements, Sam decided "triangulation" was necessary to identify accurate transfer information to meet his goals. He found the resources he needed, including specific engineering transfer guides and admission requirements, on the university's website. Armed with that information, he checked with CCC advisors and university admissions staff to confirm that he was on track as he took his coursework. Rather than rely on any one staff member, he paid close attention to information he "heard from more than one source," which he took as an indication that the information was accurate. Regardless of their primary sources of information, successful resource curators were those who found a way to analyze the information they gathered to identify common themes or "correct" information as a means of avoiding costly missteps. In Sam's case, he was able to weed out misleading information and follow the transfer guide in his specific program of interest at a flagship institution; he transferred into that school's electrical engineering program during the second year of the study.

Other resource curators reported that advising staff sometimes offered "cookie-cutter" transfer plans that did not align with their specific transfer goals and priorities. Bridget, an older student at FCCS, noticed that her initial advisor did not focus on efficiency or customize advice for her transfer goals, despite Bridget's having stated her preference to "save time and money." For example, Bridget noted that the advisor had not mentioned that she could save "a whole semester of tuition at a four-year university" by taking classes at the community college that a prospective university would count as equivalents. Bridget concluded: "You have to be proactive on your own and seek out the information rather than just waiting for someone to spoon-feed you." From that point on, she carefully studied materials from several universities' websites, attended information sessions and "campus days" to get information directly from university representatives, and relied on her preferred advisor, who "not only answered questions but offered suggestions." She emphasized the role that students needed to play in that process in efforts to meet their own priorities: "I know it's a lot of information, but I think whenever there's a discussion of transfer, it should be encouraged that the student at the very least compare the coursework and then see what coursework–if it's parallel–can be done prior to transfer." Resource curators typically determined that they could not take any given piece of transfer information at face value and instead triangulated across sources to identify accurate transfer information. In this way, resource curators, despite their limited power, used the resources available to them to improve their probability of transferring. Like many other resource curators, Bridget gathered sufficient information to understand the requirements and pathways toward her transfer goal. Despite having that information, by the end of our study, she was no longer enrolled in college because of competing family obligations, though she still hoped to transfer to a university and continue working toward her baccalaureate degree in business.

The process of keeping track of transfer information obtained from various sources could be tedious and time consuming. Dolores, a student at CCC, described, in the first year of the study, her organizational system for keeping track of transfer information and fact-checking it through the advisors at her college: "I have an Excel sheet that I keep. Those transfer sheets, I just make sure . . . , if I want to get into a college, that I am following all [the requirements]. I just had little lists and stuff." She followed up regularly with advising staff to check her interpretation of those requirements and to confirm she was on track. She explained:

> I have all the transfer sheets. I pretty much compare everything. I talk to the CCC counselor here at least once a month. They should give me a job here, because I am always bugging them. They are like, "No, it is our job." I am just like, "No, I need to figure out what I am doing." A lot of people just stay at CCC and just get their associate or they just quit in general. I just want to make sure I have the path of least resistance right now to go to a university.

For Dolores, the path of least resistance for transferring required a big investment of her time and effort; she planned out her coursework semesters in advance, regularly confirmed that her grades and courses would meet the requirements of prospective institutions, and attended transfer events and sessions for those institutions. Once she had settled on a destination university, she kept a constant watch on how her courses would transfer: "I audited myself maybe an unhealthy amount of times just to make sure all the classes at [CCC] counted towards my university degree, so I didn't really have many surprises." In addition to meeting with advisors at CCC, she checked in with the recruiter and with a counselor at her destination university to confirm how credits would apply toward her bachelor's degree. When she transferred to a regional university in the middle of year two of the study, "all [her] credits transferred to the degree plan," allowing her to enter with junior status. She emphasized her vigilance about degree plans and transfer requirements at prospective universities, coupled with her seeking confirmation from actors at both the community college and the university, as essential for staying on track throughout the process. She earned her bachelor's degree, with a double major, after three years at the university.

Because resource curators sought to adhere to the rules and norms of the transfer field, most resource curators—80 percent—were sufficiently informed about transfer pathways and the steps they needed to take to reach their educational goals. Given the competing requirements across degree programs at a given community college and different destination universities, collecting information from multiple sources was vital to being sufficiently informed to pursue transfer. Resource curators gained advantage in the transfer field by gathering as much information as they could and finding ways to triangulate so that they could troubleshoot misaligned information. Yet even resource curator students were not guaranteed success, particularly if they did not identify strategies for identifying and eliminating misinformation. Some resource curators—20 percent of them—were informed but misguided. Even those who invested time and energy into resource curation sometimes missed key insights or were unable to identify the correct transfer plan when faced with a complex web of information. But by the end of our study, 83 percent of resource curators had transferred.

Hesitant Advisees

Hesitant advisees, like resource curators, worked to find their own information about transfer procedures and requirements, but unlike resource curators, hesitant advisees who found their community college advisors to be unhelpful or to offer inaccurate information eschewed advisors. About 21 percent of students were hesitant advisees, making this the second most common information-gathering approach among students in our sample.

Hesitant advisees failed to find an institutional actor at their college to help them sort through transfer information. In many cases, students perpetually decided not to visit advisors because they felt unprepared to ask for advice or weren't sure of what they could expect of their advisors. When asked whether he had talked to any advisors about transferring, Tony, an FCCS student, said: "Honestly, no. I haven't talked to anybody." He noted that the structure of his college's advising, where he did not have one stable advisor, contributed to his hesitation: "Part of the problem is that they have been switching advisors. It doesn't seem like I have one specific advisor that I have here in the time that I have been. I think I am actually on my third. I haven't talked to her face-to-face or had an interview with her." The revolving door of advisors made Tony feel like it wasn't worthwhile to connect with advising staff about transfer and made it harder to develop trusting relationships. In fact, the only people at his college he had spoken to about transferring were peers, who also had no experience with transfer. As a first-generation college student, Tony had greater difficulty in accessing the information and knowledge he needed to navigate transfer. He noted, "Most of my peers, they either didn't go to a four-year university or—there's not really anybody that I know" that had attended a university, other than one cousin. Like several other hesitant advisees, Tony explained that he wanted to be ready to list his goals and questions before he visited an advisor to talk about transferring. By year three, the last time we spoke with him, he was no longer enrolled in college because of external challenges that included financial constraints and a health crisis. He hoped to transfer at some point in the future, though he was still unclear about what steps he would need to take to achieve his goal.

Other hesitant advisees actively avoided advisors, typically in response to a previous bad experience with advising staff. Each of these students noted having had an encounter that led them to receive incorrect transfer information. One student, Steven, described his lackluster experiences with advisors at CCC thus: "There is nobody I have found that is my guru or something—an advisor that I am just like 'I have to go to the person!' I am sure there are plenty of great advisors. But I have had one at [this campus] that I wasn't too satisfied with. So I probably won't go back." He noted that the advice he received from the advisor was too broad to be helpful in navigating the specifics of transfer between institutions. Steven now preferred to talk to colleagues or friends because, he said:

> Honestly, I think I get better information from a colleague, or associate, or I don't know, a contemporary, peer. I don't know the right word, but she's at [the university] already. She transferred about a year ago, I think. Maybe it was a little bit more than a year ago, but she works with me, and so I ask her questions about stuff like [credit transfer], because the

> CCC counselors, they don't really know what they're talking about as far as what transfers, and I don't know. . . . It's like you got to kind of be in the know, and that's just something that I've developed over time and experience. . . . Most of my information I get from peers, the internet sometimes, researching stuff, and then Phi Theta Kappa, an honor society that I'm a member of, and going to those meetings has helped a lot with me understanding certain things about scholarships and stuff like that. So I guess in a way I've just kind of had to figure it out on my own with little bit of help here and there.

He reported visiting an advisor only when "it is critical," for example, to have an advising bar (an administrative hold that would prevent registration until he met with an advisor) removed. To get information about transferring, Steven turned to faculty, friends, coworkers, and customers at the grocery store where he worked, which was near the university he wanted to attend. Given his access to several peers who had attended college, Steven was able to gather sufficient information to successfully navigate transfer; he enrolled at the flagship university after two years at the community college.

Several hesitant advisees voiced their frustrations regarding incorrect and inconsistent advice from advisors. Mona, a student at FCCS, explained that in her first semester of college, she visited her assigned advisor and told them which degree she wanted to earn. She followed the degree plan they gave her and "ended up taking a couple courses that [she] didn't need for that program." After she "learned about finding the plans online," she decided, "I don't need you anymore, and I can do this myself. . . . I want to know what I'm doing." Indeed, Mona successfully transferred after two years, following the degree plan, despite having actively avoided advisors. Hesitant advisees typically concluded that, compared with their experience of self-guiding through transfer information, visiting advisors "just didn't seem as effective," as Mona put it.

Most hesitant advisees built sufficient information to navigate transfer, though students in this subgroup were dispersed across all three information tracks. We identified more than half—58 percent—as having sufficient information to achieve their transfer goals through self-advising. The remaining hesitant students were primarily underinformed (33 percent), and one student was informed but misguided. Hesitant advisees were most successful when they found actors to rely on within the field—often university admissions staff—rather than only external actors. Hesitant advisees who were underinformed or informed but misguided failed to identify trustworthy and useful sources of transfer information. They largely relied on noninstitutional actors (people outside of the field) but struggled to gather accurate transfer information because institutional actors were more familiar with the field's rules and norms. After six years, 83 percent of hesitant advisee students transferred—a rate similar to that observed among resource curators.

System Trusters

In contrast to the hesitant advisees, system trusters—who made up 12 percent of students in the sample—put a lot of faith in advising staff to lead them through the rules and requirements for transfer without consulting other resources. In many cases, they received a transfer or degree plan and adhered to it, sometimes despite their own uncertainty. Students we describe as system trusters had clear expectations of the roles advisors should play and did not seem to encounter advisors who violated these norms. Carmen, a first-generation college student and mother of two children, described the advisors at CCC as "really good about helping you decide where to go." She elaborated: "I'm going to go with them because they've got my information. They know my work ethic. I think they'll be able to help me find the best school for me." Carmen relied on the information they provided and did not do any additional research. She planned to enroll in CCC's bachelor's degree program in nursing. Transitioning into the program didn't require coordinating across institutions, which made it easier for her to rely on information from her community college advisors. The information she received was sufficient, and she had completed her associate degree and transferred to the bachelor's program by her fourth year in the study.

Other students similarly followed the plan laid out by their advisors. Hannah, an FCCS student who wanted to transfer in business, said that her advisor typically provided the information she requested, such as transfer guides and information for different universities, noting, "She gave me a scope of what my focus needed to be." Although Hannah was satisfied with her advisor, she also realized that her advisor never provided information beyond what she explicitly requested. Hannah pondered whether she should be getting more from the experience: "I pretty much just asked about [two local universities]. She gave me what I asked for on [one of them]. . . . I guess I should have, or could have, asked her opinion on various other universities. I didn't really get, I guess, research on pursuing a degree at [others], so I'm just sticking with [the one she gave me]. . . . I guess I should have, or could have, asked her opinion on various other universities."

Hannah explained that she had narrowed her scope because her advisor had given her information about only that college. At the same time, she put the responsibility on herself to explicitly ask about transfer options. She said, "I could get her feedback on weighing the options and determining the best option for me. I should ask." Ultimately, Hannah did not have the capacity to conduct additional research, in part because of her family responsibilities (she had three children of her own and two other teenage family members to care for). She completed her associate degree but decided not to pursue transfer.

Other system trusters acknowledged that their conversations with advisors typically did not include a discussion of their overall career goals, which meant the information they received was specific to their immediate inquiry rather than tailored to their long-term goals. Students we classified as trusters did not consult other sources about their options—their information was shaped almost entirely by advising staff. Putting such faith in advisors alone for transfer guidance put trusters at risk of receiving misinformation, particularly if the advisors relied on out-of-date information or transfer plans. Even though the advisors we spoke to were well intentioned and generally took a student-centered approach, they also described a context with constantly changing policies, admission standards, and procedures that made it difficult to keep up with new information. System trusters yielded power and authority to their advisors, unaware that the existing norms and values advisors implement focus more on preserving university authority than on fostering student access and success.

System trusters typically followed the steps laid out by their advisor. If the advisor were familiar with the student's specific goal and well versed in various transfer pathways, the student could receive sufficient information to transfer. This was the case for 57 percent of our trusters. The remainder were underinformed (29 percent) and informed but misguided (14 percent). Because they exercised less agency in the process than resource curators and hesitant advisees, trusters risked being underinformed if their advisors provided them with a degree plan that did not align with their desired major and degree; they were often unsure of which plan they were on. Trusters were also less likely to check requirements against college websites or to reach out to four-year staff—in other words, they often failed to triangulate across sources. One student, Hortensia, explained to us that she had "pretty much accomplished everything" on her degree plan, but as we probed, it became clear that she was following a degree plan that did not align with her desired program for transfer. Despite her confidence in the plan her advisor had given her (which was for a technical associate degree rather than an academic program with credits that would transfer to her desired bachelor's degree), the bulk of the credits would not transfer. Later, by year four, she recognized that she had received inaccurate information from her initial advisor. When we asked whether she trusted the information from her new advisor, she said: "I mean, I had to trust it. I didn't have any other choice . . . I think I had a lot of faith in her. . . . After I found her as an advisor, I think I was really comfortable, and I just kind of trusted her word." Despite her negative experience with an earlier advisor, Hortensia continued to have great trust in the advising staff. Because of the misinformation she received from her advising interactions, she later had to obtain two associate degrees—one technical and one academic. She had put her transfer plan on hold but still hoped to transfer eventually.

Overall, only 30 percent of system trusters had transferred by the end of our study, illustrating how essential it is to gather additional resources—outside of advising—in a system that places the responsibility on implementing students to follow transfer rules and norms.

Disconnected Students

The final theme we observed among student implementers was often demonstrated by students who lacked clear goals for transfer regarding either major or destination institution and did not seek information to move toward their transfer aspirations. Disconnected students haphazardly received information from staff or peers without pursuing information on their own. Rather than seek to learn the "rules of the game" to navigate transfer, these students largely seemed unaware of the transfer field or of their position in the field. Only 7 percent of students in our sample fit this profile.

Disconnected students often changed their mind about their major or transfer institution without researching transfer options, and they were easily swayed by information that came their way. Gina, for example, entered FCCS in a collision technology certificate program but wanted to transfer to a four-year institution in a different major. She was uncertain about her preferred field of study, torn between kinesiology and music education—neither of which aligned with her current (and still accruing) credits in collision technology. Her most frequent staff interaction at FCCS was with a program advisor in the collision technology program who recommended that she focus on the certificate program, which was not eligible for transfer (technical credits cannot transfer to an academic baccalaureate in Texas) and did not overlap with Gina's preferred majors. Gina did not sign up to visit an advisor or look for transfer guides or degree plans in her desired majors. At the same time, no one at her institution encouraged her to visit the advising office, despite the misalignment between her program and her stated goals. In the first several years of our study, Gina was underinformed about transfer options and requirements but determined to transfer despite the lack of alignment between her goals and many of her courses at FCCS. She decided to transfer to a local university after three years at the community college and eventually went on to earn her bachelor's degree in kinesiology. Gina described losing a substantial number of credits when she transferred; she had realized midsemester that "I was pretty much taking this class for nothing" but nevertheless decided to "stick it out." Those courses ended up contributing to excess elective credits.

When exposed to transfer information, disconnected students were easily influenced by it but struggled to move forward—often because they experienced minimal intervention from community college staff, who expected them to do the research on their own. One student at FCCS, Benito, described learning about options to transfer into a bachelor's program in applied science from a university recruiter who was visiting FCCS: "I saw a spokesperson for A&M, the people who go out and talk to the schools and try to get people to transfer." Through this interaction, Benito became interested in transferring there before he had information about how the program aligned with his current program. Initially he said, "I haven't really done all that [looked at websites or talked to an advisor]. It should be pretty easy. But I haven't really looked online or anything." When he met with the FCCS advisor, the meeting was "just to see what classes [I was] going to take the following semester." The advisor did not bring up transfer options with Benito, and he did not explicitly ask for that information. Operating with only the initial information from the recruiter, Benito felt overwhelmed by trying to figure out the details. By the end of the third year of the study, he said, he felt that transferring seemed "like too much right now" and had decided to delay.

By the end of our follow-up (six years after we initially met him), Benito had not transferred and still noted that he was interested in doing so. When he finally requested transfer information from FCCS advisors, he was bewildered upon learning that not all of his classes would count toward a degree if he transferred: "I had no idea all the credits don't transfer. I thought it was something that goes everywhere. I thought everything transferred. I didn't know some things don't transfer." We asked whether, in those meetings, he had received information about which credits would transfer to which programs (i.e., Were some degree plans and programs willing to accept more of his credits?). He could not offer specifics and replied: "They told me the same thing pretty much, that not everything would transfer, but some do. [They talked about] how to earn other degrees at the other school, what I need to do to earn it." Overall, it seemed as if Benito was missing specific information about which transfer pathway would take more of his accumulated credits and which aligned best with his career and educational goals.

The lack of staff outreach to transfer-intending students about transfer options was a defining feature of the experience of disconnected students. Because students were expected to, essentially, *opt in* to transfer advising, those who did not proactively request information about potential transfer pathways did not receive any advice about them. Another disconnected student, Scarlet, lamented this lack of outreach: "I think at the community college level you have to do a little more digging in terms of finding out this kind of thing. I think I would like a little more information being provided to me." When we followed up with her several years later, she still felt frustrated by her advising relationship; she described advisors as "doing a pretty good job of answering questions" but said she thought transfer guidance shouldn't be based only on her taking initiative and asking specific questions. She observed:

> I think they should be helping to direct the students a little bit more. Like, instead of just saying, "These are what are required in order to graduate. You have to take one of these classes," I think it should be a little more tailored to say, "Okay, based on whether you're going full time or part time or what your transfer goals are, it's recommended that maybe you start up by trying to balance your courses and don't take, you know, all major courses in one semester."

Scarlet believed that advisors at the community college should take what she described as a more "caring" approach, intervening to check in with her about her educational goals and using their professional expertise to guide her in course selection toward those goals. Scarlet was underinformed about her transfer options and took a circuitous path, often shifting her plans when exposed to new information. The information she received most consistently was offered by her family members (her father had attended her target destination university, one of the state flagships); she did not experience (nor did she pursue) consistent advising at CCC. After several years of attending CCC and shifting between full- and part-time enrollment, she finally applied to transfer during year six of the study and learned she was admitted later that spring.

In many ways, the disconnected students we followed felt as though they had fallen through the cracks at their community college. They aimed to transfer but reported that no one at their institution followed up with them to ensure they were on the path toward that goal. Without structured supports, they felt unsure of what steps to take and were easily swayed—and at times misled—by the pieces of information they came across. Disconnected students were equally likely to end up underinformed about transfer pathways, or informed but misguided. Because they haphazardly received information from different sources for various goals or institutions, these students often ended up with insufficient information for any specific pathway, given inadequate advising and their lack of institutional connections. These students appeared unaware of the rules of the transfer field and did not obtain quality transfer information, largely because they were disconnected from institutional actors. By the end of our study, three-fourths of disconnected students had not transferred but still intended to earn a bachelor's degree.

Navigating Complex Information in the Transfer Field: Understanding the Burden Placed on Transfer-Intending Students

Our findings from the previous chapters illustrate how personnel at Texas community colleges and universities created and maintained shared rules and norms related to community college transfer. We followed transfer-intending community college students over six years, observing the consequences of field rules and norms for their behavior and transfer success. Like community college staff, students serve as dominated actors, where the actions available to them are merely to implement the field rules, which primarily serve to maintain the standards set by universities. Students have to invest time and energy to gather information about transfer pathways and policies as their primary means of meeting their educational aspirations. The complex structure of information—wherein each institution provides its own transfer information and resources, with little collaboration and minimal alignment—systematically disadvantages community college students.

As implementers, community college students faced difficulty performing the actions expected of their role. In a field where university actors determine how credits apply toward bachelor's programs and are primarily responsible for information dissemination, finding and vetting transfer information was at times so difficult that even community college staff were unsure whether they had accurate information. In fact, both community college and university personnel argued that students could not rely on community college advising alone to be sufficiently informed about transfer—they had to gather additional information and triangulate across multiple sources.

Given this emphasis on the student role in transfer-information curation, student implementers were often confused about what to expect of advisors. They scrambled to make sense of transfer information upon receiving inaccurate or incomplete information from advising staff. Some of them noticed that advisors' priorities and motives conflicted with their own, particularly when it came to encouraging students to complete the state's core curriculum—the "basics," as many students and staff referred to core courses—or an associate degree prior to transfer. These conflicts left them confused and, at times, unsure of how best to proceed, as was the case for Teresa as she tried to determine whether to earn an associate degree before transferring. When it became clear that not all advisors provided tailored and accurate advice aligned with students' interests, some students (hesitant advisees) refrained from interacting with advisors, turning instead to friends, institutional websites, or, occasionally, university recruiters. Successful resource curators relied on resources outside of the community college, analyzing information from several sources to identify common themes. In this way, resource curators, despite their limited power, sought to improve their positions in the transfer field to maximize their chance of transfer.

Students who primarily entrusted their advisor with providing transfer information reinforced the authority of their advisors, who, even if begrudgingly, worked to reify existing norms and values that focused more on preserving university authority than on fostering student success. System trusters who were provided with the wrong transfer guide by staff were unlikely to gain sufficient transfer information. They did not seek outside information—it is possible that they lacked the social capital to do so—and therefore risked making costly missteps, including accumulating credits that would not count toward their desired degree. Some students, particularly those disconnected from the field, failed to perform actions expected of them. These students were unclear about the rules and norms of the field, which left them more susceptible to being misinformed or underinformed and therefore less likely to transfer. They often expected an advisor to intervene if there were steps they should take toward their transfer goals, but the field was not set up to offer those interventions, as most advisors emphasized that students needed to ask for transfer information to receive it.

Overall, students who used information-gathering approaches that did not seek information or resources outside of their college (system trusters and disconnected students) were much less likely to end up with sufficient transfer information and had substantially lower rates of transfer than their peers. Among students who took on the burden of curating resources (resource curators and hesitant advisees), rates of transfer were more than 80 percent by the end of the study. At the same time, even among students who dedicated substantial time and energy to gathering information about transfer—recall the elaborate spreadsheets and lists that several students created to keep track of transfer options and requirements—17 percent of students ultimately did not transfer (all of those students, at our last interview with them, still aspired to earn a bachelor's degree). Even those with sufficient information are not guaranteed success. In some cases, as we saw with Bridget, external factors threw them off course.

The challenges students in our sample faced in navigating transfer information underscore the burden placed on community college students. The hurdles community college students encounter when gathering information are compounded by competing external financial and familial obligations. External life events—such as family obligations or the need to work for pay full time—thwarted some students' plans. For students from low-income families and with external obligations, elaborate information-seeking approaches are often an additional burden that they cannot take on. Yet these are the students who stand to benefit the most from a bachelor's degree. Claudia, an FCCS student who was working full time and helping to raise her granddaughter, described the challenges she faced in navigating higher education: "I work forty-five hours a week, and the baby and my home life and, and, and, and. . . . There's just too much. I couldn't do it." By the end of year six of the study, she had taken a break from schooling but still aimed to transfer to a local university someday, concluding that it would take longer than she had anticipated.

The decentralized nature of the higher education system and the variation in transfer information provided across institutions place the burden on students to familiarize themselves with transfer options. In chapter 5, we further distill the themes from our results, describing the roles and priorities of various actors within the transfer field. Then we consider the implications for higher education stakeholders and potential ways to improve—and overhaul—the transfer field.

CHAPTER 5

Shifting the Field of Transfer

Implications and Steps Forward

Community colleges, with their relatively low cost and open-access mission, can broaden postsecondary opportunities, especially for the most marginalized students. Many baccalaureate-aspiring students in the United States begin higher education at a community college, yet many do not transfer or complete a bachelor's degree, which creates a tension in public policy discussions about both how to invest in these institutions and how to resolve the ineffective transfer system in public higher education. In this book, we sought to explore the tension between the promise of community colleges to broaden postsecondary access and the low rates of transfer.

Previous research has, rightly, pointed to inefficiencies, lack of resources, and complex organization of community colleges as sources of the transfer problem.[1] Community colleges, with their broad missions, attempt to provide something for everyone, so they offer many different courses, degrees, and certificate programs, not all of which are transferable to a university. Degree pathways are often unstructured—a "shapeless river"—which means that students can easily be diverted from their goals and end up taking courses that don't contribute to their degree.[2] Community colleges have invested in advising supports to help students navigate transfer, but at many institutions, the high advising loads make offering individualized support for all students untenable.

Critiques of community colleges, and persuasive reforms like Guided Pathways, have led to major investments in restructuring program pathways, exploring new advising approaches, and providing other supports for community college students.[3] These approaches are all reasonable and laudable efforts, as we discuss further below; yet most of the research and strategies have focused on the structure of community colleges as organizations, neglecting how they are situated within a broader sociopolitical *field*. We highlight the critical interactions between organizations, especially the disproportionate power of universities, that shape the field of transfer and thereby create barriers for students in their pursuit of their educational aspirations.

Reframing the Problem of Transfer and Finding a Path Forward

In this chapter, we summarize our key findings and consider the implications for higher education institutions. Drawing on six years of longitudinal interview data with transfer-intending students and personnel at Texas community colleges and public universities, we illustrate that improving vertical transfer requires a fundamental shift in how we think about the "transfer problem." That shift consists of moving from viewing the issue as a *community college problem* to seeing it as a *public higher education problem*. By taking a field-level approach, we expose the underlying power dynamics that create and perpetuate unequal opportunities in higher education. Rather than place responsibility for transfer outcomes on either the student or the community college actors—as many of the previous efforts have done—we show that individual actions are shaped by a broader set of rules and norms. By uncovering specific ways that the transfer system fails students, our research identifies critical leverage points for smoothing transfer processes and improving outcomes. In this chapter, we draw on our findings to consider potential ways to intervene in ineffective transfer systems. We describe a path forward toward simplified transfer for students and compromise for institutions and policy makers.

One of our major findings was that university actors played a significant—and often unexplored—role in shaping the field of transfer. These dominant actors sought to maintain the status quo, including the element of how their discretion over how credits would apply after transfer, which often thwarted state policies that could smooth and streamline transfer for students. The behavior of university actors regarding credit transfer and admissions was focused primarily on preserving institutional (and program) privilege and prestige. No university actors we spoke to expressed intention to exacerbate inequities in educational access, but their role in the transfer field ultimately served to reproduce broader societal inequality in degree attainment across race and class by shifting administrative burdens from the state (or institutions) to individuals.[4]

Given the uneven power structures across institutions, community college actors in our study often implemented the field's existing norms, policies, and procedures—rules that were determined by universities. Our results suggest that through their power over curricula, university faculty shaped rules for credit transfer and applicability. That dynamic resulted in varied requirements across institutions and a complex web of information that would need to be consistently updated and disseminated among community college staff to inform transfer-seeking students. Although some community college staff did voice frustration with current transfer systems and attempted to push back to better assist students, community college staff were "not the agents of change," as noted by Lloyd, a professor and advisor at FFCS. Their action is constrained by the power dynamics in the broader field and, specifically, by the power of university faculty and staff. Although our results are in line with previous research documenting structural challenges in community colleges, our findings illustrate how the existing social order in higher education complicates students' ability to navigate transfer. These field-level dynamics offer insights—and raise some questions—about what we may expect from large-scale reforms intended for community colleges. Overall, our findings suggest a need to look beyond the walls of the community college.

When public institutions in the broader postsecondary environment fail to elucidate transfer pathways, they create unique challenges that require students to curate information from various sources. For students from low-income families and with external obligations, elaborate information-seeking approaches are an additional burden that they cannot take on. Yet these are the students who stand to benefit the most from a bachelor's degree. The rules of the field thus have the potential to compound the disadvantages faced by the most marginalized students in the postsecondary system.

We found that even if students simply followed the advice of community college staff, they could be led astray because it was virtually impossible for staff to keep up with the vast amount of transfer information, which was constantly changing. This means that even students with "sufficient information" are not guaranteed success. Although improved transfer information and guides could help them, our findings suggest that narrow policy fixes focused on information alone will not solve the transfer problem.

Why Existing Reforms Will Not Be Enough

Examining field-level dynamics helps shed light on how existing or proposed reforms to improve transfer may play out. Whole-college reforms at community colleges, such as changes recommended by the Guided Pathways movement, aim to disrupt the status quo. Guided Pathways reforms focus largely on community colleges. Although they may be effective at shifting processes and structures within those institutions, the reforms may be ineffective at improving baccalaureate attainment if *only* community colleges undertake them. Without parallel reforms at the public universities, the most powerful players in the transfer field—incumbents at universities—will likely still adhere to the original rules and norms. This would leave intermediaries (community college advisors and administrators) and those with the least power (transfer-intending students) in the same dominated position they currently experience. A next wave of pathway reforms would need to involve public universities to create transparent transfer pathways to a baccalaureate.

Other interventions inspired by behavioral science that focus on informational reforms, such as intrusive advising and "nudges" to incentivize certain behaviors, may be palatable to actors at various positions in the field because of their low cost and easy implementation.[5] For example, such strategies may include texting studies that nudge students to meet with their advisor or to visit their college's transfer information website to learn more about transfer procedures or which courses should apply toward a degree at various destination universities. These interventions are palatable because they are fairly painless: they allow universities to keep their institutional autonomy. By emphasizing better informing and guiding students through byzantine processes and policies, the informational interventions provide information without altering the status quo. The problem is that information-reform approaches are error prone. They rely on individuals to constantly update information for external institutional actors and students, leaving several stages in the information pipeline, where the flow can break down. For instance, who is responsible for updating information, and through which platforms? How frequently will changes be communicated, and with which partners? Then how will personnel at partnering institutions ensure that updates are shared with students?

In many ways, the existing state policies in Texas follow an information-reform approach. For example, a recent policy required public institutions in Texas to post their recommended course sequences on public websites, which should mean required courses are more transparent for transfer-intending students.[6] But this policy assumes that those required course sequences are accurate, usable, and up to date, and it relies on students—and those who guide them—to know about and make use of that information. Texas state policies also include a transferable core of lower-division courses (the core curriculum), which, under the recent Texas Transfer Framework, should combine with additional major-specific courses (Field of Study curricula) to count toward a degree at another institution and "universal" course numbering for lower-division courses. Unfortunately, in practice, implementation of the policies can be spotty, and accountability for compliance appears nonexistent, especially for the more comprehensive initiatives like the Texas Transfer Framework. Universal course numbering in the state is not truly universal, given that it is mandated only for the community colleges and that most universities—other than the most transfer-receptive ones—do not use it. Transfer-intending students must go through the additional step of translating course numbers across institutions.

These policies seek to simplify information to help students translate how their credits will move across institutions, but none of these policies guarantee what will happen on the back end, once students arrive at the university. There are no systematic accountability measures in place to ensure university actors apply credits from an origin institution toward a degree in a related field, even under conditions like the Field of Study agreement, which technically should require universities to do so (students can, at best, file a complaint with the coordinating board, if they figure out how to do so). As a result, students can still end up with excess credits, despite using the best available information. Thus, policies that maintain universities' power over information and credit transfer processes ultimately maintain a system in which community college students are systematically disadvantaged. In the absence of more stringent government intervention and accountability, these strategies allow universities to continue with business as usual and put community college baccalaureate aspirants at a considerable disadvantage.

Policy Recommendations: How Can State Governments Intervene?

We anticipate that the most likely case for change would come from government mandates. Government intervention, in which university actors are compelled to enact new policies—such as adopting a transferable associate degree or a policy that guarantees lower-division coursework aligned with the posttransfer major will apply toward a degree (like the Texas Transfer Framework, but with accountability for universities)—could shift the social order. Centralized and institutionalized policies, systems, and structures implemented to support such mandates would limit the burden on individual students to gather information, fill out paperwork, and navigate the transfer system.

Research on community college transfer suggests that the student experiences we captured, where students must deliberate across policy signals from various sources, are not unique to Texas. Studies that describe effective transfer partnerships emphasize the importance of well-articulated transfer curricula and outreach among staff at four-year institutions to clarify whether and how they accept credits upon transfer, even in contexts with more centralized transfer articulation and the presence of statewide transfer agreements.[7] Too often, however, the target of "the problem" has been community colleges; this emphasis misses the bigger picture and obscures the other actors who shape the rules of the game. Our findings and implications, particularly the need for heavy-handed policy to force changes in the status quo and to realign power structures, have implications for other states seeking to improve transfer outcomes.

In state contexts in which students appear overly burdened to curate resources to effectively navigate credit transfer, we advocate for the adoption of a policy under which an associate degree guarantees admission in the same major to at least one public university, where institutions must apply the sixty credits toward the bachelor's degree and count students as having completed their general education core (so that transfer students can focus on major-specific courses). Under such a policy, universities must accept general education and premajor courses to the extent that doing so allows for junior standing in the same major, but *how* they accept and substitute courses is otherwise up to them (meaning some institutional/departmental autonomy is maintained). This approach places the burden on the receiving institution and department (rather than on students, as is the case under the status quo) to decide how credits will substitute (avoiding excess elective credits for students) and to attempt to anticipate what those decisions will look like (departments would be incentivized to inform prospective students of course equivalencies). Even in states that have moved forward with guaranteed transfer for associate degree recipients, like California, *accountability for those policies is essential*; government actors must follow up with destination institutions to make sure credits transfer as mandated.

We expect that mandates for lower-division credits to apply toward a degree in the same field would improve clarity for students better than any information-based approach, but we suspect that some actors in the public higher education system would not find such mandates palatable. One potential repercussion may be that selective institutions would decide to accept fewer transfer students (but at the same time, at least in the Texas context, that trend is happening anyway, without any corresponding benefits for students). Therefore, this approach may require greater communication to improve buy-in among universities, perhaps by emphasizing the alignment with their goals of increasing diversity and equity. Given that community colleges disproportionately serve Black and Hispanic students and students from families of lower socioeconomic status, admitting more transfer students could increase racial and socioeconomic diversity—an institutional priority likely to take on new importance in the post–affirmative action era.

How do we move toward those reforms? Such efforts need not be led by challengers—the relatively weak community college actors—but by "transfer-receptive" universities.[8] If transfer-receptive universities work with legislators and the coordinating board to push transfer reforms, the field's power dynamics may shift. The most selective, least transfer-receptive institutions may push back against those efforts. If necessary, states could exclude more selective institutions from the mandate (as originally occurred with the California State University system adopting an associate degree that transferred before the University of California also took on a similar "associate degree with a guarantee" policy). In Texas contexts, the most oversubscribed flagships—University of

Texas at Austin and Texas A&M University College Station—are already subject to a top-10-percent rule and, because of demand, can admit only the top 6 percent of graduating high school students to each school. If they are omitted from such a policy based purely on a lack of political will, students who transfer there need to be cautious given the potential for credit loss. At the same time, such an exception seems unnecessary, as both institutions take a small fraction of the transfer population and would only be subject to following transfer directives like the Texas Transfer Framework or a guaranteed associate degree in cases where their own admission staff determined the students were worthy of admission.

Recommendations for Practice: Improving Institutional Processes with Field-Level Insights

Although the shortcomings of transfer processes in many states will most likely need to be addressed by state policies, institutional policies and practices may also help to improve transfer outcomes for students. Here we discuss how our findings can inform practices in community colleges and universities to improve students' experiences of navigating transfer.

We found that the community colleges in our study had many of the same structural challenges documented in the broader literature. They faced high rates of staff and faculty turnover, high advisee-student ratios, and complex degree and credential pathways and course requirements. As a result, students reported experiencing uneven advising at community colleges. We argue that community colleges have already borne the brunt of pressures to reform and improve transfer mechanisms, but our findings do point to some advising and support systems at community colleges that can help.

For example, strong advising is an excellent way to supplement existing sources of information; it can help or hinder students' paths to transfer success. Advising seemed to be the most helpful to our students when it connected them to university resources.[9] In the Texas context, given the power of universities to shape transfer outcomes, it was important for students to connect with university staff before transferring to understand transfer and major requirements. We therefore also recommend that community colleges continue or expand opportunities to connect with university representatives through existing structures, such as transfer fairs. Transfer fairs hosted by community colleges are instrumental in connecting students with their target universities and provide an opportunity for students to meet with university staff in person.

Although advising did help some of our students transfer, the advising experiences of *hesitant advisees*—such as Tony, who visited advisors occasionally but did not find them useful—show that not all advising interactions are created equal. We therefore recommend using high-touch advising practices to communicate with students early on in their college experience about their educational goals and ensure they receive transfer information from the beginning; even students who note that they are unsure of their final educational goal should be made aware of transfer resources offered at their institution. Doing so can help reduce the number of negative experiences of our students in the *disconnected* category, like Benito and Gina. Receiving transfer information should not require opting in and preparing a list of specific questions. Perhaps providing additional advisor training or a set protocol at each institution that would encourage advisors to inquire about what students may be looking for in a destination university could initiate student-advisor conversations about transfer instead of waiting for students to take the initiative in leading them. Otherwise, the least advantaged students are likely to remain disconnected from essential transfer services and advice.

Our work also has implications for how community colleges partner with university actors. Even within the context of this power structure, community colleges can form partnerships and regional collaborations, like the one we describe in chapter 3, with transfer-receptive universities. Although the research literature contains some useful extant guidance about building transfer partnerships, regional collaborations can be challenging to scale—especially when powerful universities are involved—and cannot remove challenges for students navigating the transfer process.[10] This is why we do advocate for state policy change rather than purely relying on institutional actors to enact change from the ground level. Where possible, building alliances with transfer-receptive universities can still solidify transfer pathways for students, even if universities that are less transfer receptive are unwilling to participate in those collaborations. Additionally, beyond building formal agreements, building a network of peers (recruiters and advisors) at common destination universities can mean that, in contexts in which state-level reforms have not yet been implemented or are not yet at scale, advisors at the community college will be more likely to be informed about changes to requirements and recommended course sequences, which will lower their risk of misinforming transfer-intending students.

Our study's main implications for university actors are that they would do well to work toward broader statewide changes to streamline transfer; to support, rather than resist, state policy efforts to do so; and to communicate with community college staff regularly to share any changes in processes or requirements. As university faculty ourselves, we are sympathetic to these actors' goals of preserving the integrity of a degree from their institutions and maintaining institutional standards. These efforts likely take on heightened significance in the current political context, where public universities face greater accountability, competition, and financial pressures that contribute to a sense of existential threat; they also face increased hostility toward their efforts to improve diversity, increase equity, and broaden access to higher education opportunities.[11] Yet the "quality assurance" efforts, as described by a community college administrator, that lead university actors to sometimes block or ignore efforts to create transfer agreements and guides and to resist equating courses across institutions, ultimately contribute more to gatekeeping than to building the prestige of programs.

Beyond working toward statewide policies to align transfer across institutions, there are other steps that universities can take at their institutions to improve transfer. University institutions have a shared responsibility to create targeted advising, access to campus resources, and clear transfer information to inform and empower transfer students. Universities can streamline transfer information, be transparent about which courses will and will not transfer, and make transfer advising more accessible for all transfer-intending students—not just for those with the know-how to navigate labyrinthian institutional structures. If providing access to academic advising is not feasible, universities can train their recruiters to conduct degree audits for all prospective transfer students to ensure they are transparent about which coursework will transfer so that students can make informed decisions and not face any costly surprises upon transferring.

Conclusion

Recent research and reform efforts emphasize the internal organization of community colleges and methods to improve support services for students. Although we agree that there is evidence for this structural argument, as described in chapter 1, our research—drawn from six years of data from transfer-intending community colleges students and the college and university actors tasked with supporting them—illustrates that community college transfer operates as a *field*, where knowledge of the roles of university actors is essential to understanding how and why the transfer system is failing students. Actors from multiple organizations, including community college advisors, university admissions personnel, and other staff, interact with each other and with transfer-intending students, sending a wide array of messages and creating a maze of transfer guidance. Students and transfer-related personnel interact in a complex higher education system in which institutions are tenuously linked and individual colleges defend their autonomy.

The resulting pressures, messages, and interactions within the broader postsecondary environment shape the experience of students and staff at a given community college. Tensions arise as individual colleges seek their own goals and enact their own procedures for transfer, with little regard for other institutions or for the needs of students. Implicit in many policy debates about course transfer (both at the state level and as part of institutional efforts to outline transfer articulation agreements) are the assumptions that the quality of instruction and learning is lower in a community college setting and that transfer students are academically underprepared. As we uncovered through interviews with faculty and staff, these biases and perceived hierarchies in higher education often shape transfer policy and the willingness of university actors to develop more streamlined pathways. The result is that these incorrect assumptions can lead to ineffective, inefficient, and inequitable transfer policies.

It is possible, if not likely, that enacting state- and institution-level policy change will require that the perception of faculty and administration regarding community colleges undergo a cultural shift. Perhaps parallel fights over racial equity in university admissions will pave the way for greater support of transfer from broad-access institutions in the name of maintaining diversity. But either way, a path forward to improve community college transfer requires action from public universities, both in Texas and beyond. That change—shifting from thwarting transfer to transforming transfer—can occur voluntarily or through mandated reforms, but community colleges cannot solve the transfer problem alone.

APPENDIX

Study Methods and Contexts

Over the course of six years, beginning in fall 2015, we followed 104 transfer-intending community college students who attended one of two public community college districts—Central Community College (CCC) and Fernando Community College System (FCCS) (both are pseudonyms)—in the same geographic region of Texas. We also interviewed transfer-relevant community college personnel and personnel at common destination universities to learn more about institutional policies and practices and about staff perspectives on the transfer process. We were purposeful in choosing two community college districts that were fairly close to each other geographically and offered similar postsecondary opportunities; this choice enabled us to explore trends across different sites. In each system, students can, and often do, take courses at multiple campuses, depending on their major, course availability, and the distance to home or work. We describe the focal institutions next and then provide additional information about our data collection and analysis.

Institutional Contexts

CCC is a multicampus community college system in a metropolitan area and enrolls over forty thousand students each year, 23 percent of whom receive Pell Grants.[1] At the time of our study, just under half (48.48 percent) of students at CCC were White; 29 percent were Latinx, 8.4 percent Black, 5.3 percent Asian, and 8.3 percent another race or multiracial. Many CCC students aim to transfer to the local public university, which is among the most selective universities in the state. Among students who initially entered CCC in 2012, 15 percent transferred to a university within six years (14 percent to a public university).[2] Those who transferred typically spent six fall or spring semesters at CCC before transferring. Only 8 percent of transfer students earned an associate degree before transferring, and 41 percent transferred with their core credits—the forty-two credits in the Texas core curriculum—completed. Thirty-seven percent went on to earn their bachelor's degree within six years.

CCC provides a variety of resources for students interested in transfer. Students are offered "walk-in" advising, and advising offices are open in the evenings and on Saturdays to provide flexibility to working students. The college offers transfer information through workshops, mandatory student success courses, an optional orientation, and the college's website, which includes links to available transfer guides and transfer agreements. At some of these transfer events, university representatives share information and marketing materials with students, often trying to recruit them to less-well-known institutions or, among recruiters for flagship universities, managing student expectations about admission prospects while informing students about transfer processes. Some students cited CCC's transfer events as helpful, but we observed that the events were not always well attended.

FCCS is a multicollege system in which Hispanic students constitute the racial/ethnic majority. The district served over fifty thousand students per year at the time of our data collection, with 28 percent receiving Pell Grants.[3] Latinx students were most prevalent (62 percent); 23.6 percent of students were White, 7.9 percent Black, 2.6 percent Asian, and 3 percent another race or multiracial. We sampled students from two colleges within the system. Many FCCS students transferred to one of two local public universities: an emerging research university and a regional comprehensive university. Among students who initially entered FCCS in 2012, 15 percent transferred to a university within six years (13 percent transferred to a public university).[4] Compared with students at CCC, those at FCCS spent one semester longer at the community college, for an average of slightly over seven semesters before transferring. Sixteen percent of FCCS transfer students earned an associate degree before transferring, and 58 percent transferred with their core curriculum complete. Among transfer students, 31 percent went on to earn their bachelor's degree within six years.

At the time of our study, FCCS was working to implement guided pathways reforms, which involve restructuring course offerings and guidance by grouping majors based on similar prerequisites to align lower-division coursework across related "meta-majors" while building additional student supports. As part of those efforts, FCCS increased outreach by advisors, requiring that automatic emails be sent to students when they reached certain milestones. FCCS hosts a transfer center on campus that houses transfer-specific advisors. This was different from the situation at CCC, where students primarily saw advisors who were "generalists" rather than transfer specialists.

Data Collection and Analysis

Student Interviews

We conducted initial interviews with students in the fall of 2015, recruiting students who expressed an intention to transfer to a four-year institution within the next twelve months. We recruited 104 participants in the first year through emails and tabling at the target colleges. We sought to follow up with them each fall semester over the next five years, with response rates ranging from 55 to 65 percent from years two through six (most years the response rate was about 65 percent, but many participants were less responsive during the height of the COVID-19 pandemic, which coincided with year six). We had an overall average participation among the full sample of 4.1 years of following up. The median number of years of participation was five years and the mode was six years; there were only fifteen students from year one that we never were able to follow up with again (those students pulled down the average); our overall rate for *any* follow-up was 85 percent. Our results focus on students with follow-up data, enabling us to track their experiences longitudinally. At the outset of the study, the ages of students in our sample ranged from nineteen to fifty-seven years; the average age was twenty-seven. The majority of students in the full sample identified as White

(56.3 percent), with 20 percent identifying as Black, 3 percent as Asian, and 5 percent as another race; 53 percent of the sample identified as Latinx (Latinx identification is not mutually exclusive of other racial categories). First-generation college students made up nearly 61 percent of the full sample.

We conducted semistructured interviews that lasted about sixty minutes each, during which we asked student participants about how and why they selected courses, what majors and careers they were considering, how and from whom they gathered information about transfer, and what schools they were choosing from. Each year, we updated the student interview protocol to focus on specific research questions and to adjust to capture varied outcomes at each phase of the transfer process. For example, in the first two years of the study, we mostly asked about students' transfer aspirations and their process for figuring out how to meet their transfer goals and determining which institutions they would attend. In years three to five of the study, we asked more explicitly about their interactions with institutional personnel, their knowledge of state transfer policies, and their methods to collect information to inform their transfer-related decisions and course taking. In year six, we focused on educational and labor market outcomes, given that many students had finished their degree or left college, and on their experiences during the COVID-19 pandemic.

To triangulate interviewees' responses with institutional practices (which helped us understand how to identify misinformation among student participants), we compared their description of transfer processes and requirements with those we gathered from staff and from institutional documents that included transfer guides and degree plans.

In table A.1, we describe the students featured in chapter 4, offering some additional context on their background, the analytic categories they were assigned to, and their transfer outcomes. Given the number of participants, we use exemplars in chapter 4 to offer evidence of broader patterns rather than include quotes from all participants.

Each year, we coded interviews after collection. We first developed general descriptive codes informed by the literature, capturing students' educational goals; use of various transfer resources; and knowledge of transfer processes, requirements, and policies. During a second round of coding, we created subcategories inductively. Members of the research team participated in a series of group coding training exercises to reach agreement about the application of codes. After agreement was reached, each team member coded an assigned caseload of transcripts, meeting each week to discuss and resolve questions and disagreements in code application.

Beginning in year two, we created a memo for each student, capturing different themes and synthesizing student experiences across the years. After our initial coding each year, we updated student memos to maintain a longitudinal record of their experiences, adding sections on specific topics and themes, based on research questions, that emerged over time. Each year, we also created metamatrices to explore themes in the data. The qualitative matrices allowed us to synthesize findings across students, campuses, and data sources to build or extend theory.

We derived categories for the matrices from the themes identified during coding and creating memos. Once the matrices were filled out, we typically examined the data in each matrix inductively to see which themes and categories emerged, and

Table A.1. Description of featured students

Pseudonym	Gender	First-gen	Race/ethnicity	Campus	Kids	Working for pay	Info-gathering approach	Sufficient information	Transferred	Years at CC	Years in study
Carmen	F	Y	Black, Hispanic	CCC	Y	Y	System truster	Sufficient	Y	4	5
Hortensia	F	Y	White, Hispanic	FCCS	Y	Y	System truster	Informed but misguided	N	2	6
Hannah	F	N	Black, Non-Hispanic	FCCS	Y	Y	System truster	Sufficient	N	5	6
Steven	M	N	White, Non-Hispanic	CCC	N	Y	Hesitant	Sufficient	Y	2	6
Mona	F	Y	American Indian/ Alaska Native, Hispanic	FCCS	N	Y	Hesitant	Sufficient	Y	2	6
Claudia	F	N	White, Hispanic	FCCS	Y	Y	Hesitant	Sufficient	N	4	6
Tony	M	Y	White, Hispanic	FCCS	N	Y	Hesitant	Under-informed	N	3	3
Teresa	F	Y	White, Hispanic	CCC	N	Y	Resource curator	Informed but misguided	Y	4	5

(*continued*)

Table A.1. Description of featured students (continued)

Pseudonym	Gender	First-gen	Race/ethnicity	Campus	Kids	Working for pay	Info-gathering approach	Sufficient information	Transferred	Years at CC	Years in study
Bridget	F	Y	Black, Non-Hispanic	FCCS	Y	Y	Resource curator	Sufficient	N	3	3
Maya	F	Y	White, Hispanic	FCCS	Y	Y	Resource curator	Informed but misguided	N	4	5
Dolores	F	Y	Asian, Hispanic	CCC	N	Y	Resource curator	Sufficient	Y	4	6
Sam	M	Y	White, Non-Hispanic	CCC	Y	Y	Resource curator	Sufficient	Y	2	6
Benito	M	Y	White, Hispanic	FCCS	N	Y	Discon-nected	Under-informed	N	4	5
Gina	F	Y	White, Hispanic	FCCS	N	Y	Discon-nected	Under-informed	Y	3	6
Scarlet	F	N	Black, Non-Hispanic	CCC	N	Y	Discon-nected	Informed but misguided/under-informed	Y	1	6

Notes: The table describes students who are featured in chapter 4. The "transferred" and "years at a community college" columns capture students' status up through their final year in the study, which for all participants was at least year five (several skipped a year or two and returned for a subsequent interview).

then we went back over the data to classify interviewees into those themes. After completing that process, we examined the matrices for patterns and themes within and across categories to draw out major findings. For example, using our identified themes, we categorized students into four categories based on their "information-gathering approach," or how they collected and navigated transfer information; those categories were resource curators, hesitant advisees, system trusters, and disconnected students. We also assessed whether they had obtained sufficient information to meet their transfer goal—their "information track"—by comparing student responses about transfer information they had or sought and expectations for credit transfer with documents provided by colleges about transfer policies. We identified three information tracks: sufficiently informed (had adequate information to lead toward stated transfer goal); underinformed (were lacking information); and misinformed or misguided (had information, but it was not aligned with transfer goals). Although we initially performed this analysis during year three of the study, we updated our analyses and student outcomes as we received additional follow-up data.

Staff Interviews

We conducted initial interviews with transfer-relevant personnel at the community colleges and common destination universities in the spring of 2016. We recruited staff in spring 2016 via email after searching college websites and contacting advising, admissions, and student services offices to identify personnel working on transfer-related issues. We identified additional staff based on recommendations of interviewees. In spring 2019 we performed additional interviews, following up with original participants and incorporating new participants in cases of staff turnover, to understand whether and how institutional policies and practices had shifted throughout our longitudinal data collection.

We interviewed thirteen staff members at the two community college districts, including six advisors, four advising-team leads, and three upper-level administrators. We also interviewed nineteen staff members from eleven destination universities, including seven admissions personnel (three administrators, four recruiters), five transfer-support staff in student affairs, six student affairs administrators, and one associate dean. The institutions included the two flagship universities (the most selective public universities), four emerging research universities (other R1 institutions striving to increase research productivity and funding), and five regional comprehensive universities (broad-access institutions with minimal admission requirements that draw local students).

We asked staff about the role state policies and institutional partnerships played in transfer processes, the structure of transfer services at their institution, and the transfer information students received and barriers they faced. We also collected institutional documents during interviews and retrieved those located online; those documents included transfer agreements and memoranda of understanding between institutions, transfer guides, and faculty-council notes. We attended transfer events and observed the interactions between staff and students. This additional evidence served to triangulate interviewees' responses with institutional practices. Combining insights from staff interviews, documents, and observations, we were able to understand the broader ecosystem in which transfer processes and policies are rooted, the rules and norms of the transfer field, and the ways actors in the field interact.

To offer context on the staff featured in chapters 2 and 3, we describe the quoted personnel—including their institution type, approximate title, and role in the field—in table A.2.

We initially coded the staff transcripts for broad themes, including each staff member's perception of the structure of the state's public higher education system and of their institution, institutional partnerships, the way the college provides information about transfer to students, knowledge and perceptions of state transfer policies, and institutional goals and priorities. We wrote memos and met to discuss emerging findings. As we analyzed our data, we found that it departed from prior frames in the community college literature, which focused primarily on student experiences and support structures within institutions. We sought a theoretical framework that could help us to understand the interinstitutional dynamics we observed and used strategic action fields to reanalyze our data.[5] We developed a staff-specific qualitative matrix, applying strategic action fields to our first round of coding.[6] In the matrix, we captured whether institutional actors fit the constructs of "incumbents," "governance units," or "challengers" and evidence to support that classification; their perceptions of other actors in the field; and their descriptions of the standards and norms that students and staff must follow related to transfer.

Table A.2. Description of featured staff interviewees

Pseudonym	Campus type	Title	Gender	Job description	Years in role	Role in the field
University staff						
Josh	University: Regional comprehensive 1	Director, Advising Initiatives	M	Student affairs (transfer) personnel	2	Challenger
Casey	University: Regional comprehensive 2	Director, Undergraduate Admissions	M	Admissions administrator	25	Governance unit
Don	University: Flagship 1	Assistant director, Admissions	M	Admissions recruiter	3	Governance unit
Mike	University: Flagship 1	Director, Transfer Programs	M	Administrator	15	Incumbent
Stella	University: Flagship 1	Coordinator, Transfer Programs	F	Student affairs (transfer) personnel	3	Incumbent
Ben	University: Regional comprehensive 3	Associate director, Admissions	F	Admissions administrator	6	Incumbent
Harriet	University: Striving research 1	Associate vice president, Enrollment Management	F	Administrator	13	Challenger
Chris	University: Striving research 2	Dean, Student Services	M	Administrator	5	Incumbent
Margo	University: Regional comprehensive 4	Admissions counselor, Transfer	F	Admissions recruiter	8	Challenger

Ana Lucia	University: Regional comprehensive 5	Counselor, Transfer Admissions	F	Admissions recruiter	8	Governance unit
Brian	University: Striving Research 2	Director, Advising	M	Student affairs (transfer) personnel	6	Incumbent
Eric	University: Flagship 2 (Austin)	Coordinator, Transfer Programs	M	Student affairs (transfer) personnel	1	Implementer
Kevin	University: Flagship 2	Associate director, Admissions	M	Admissions administrator	4	Governance unit
Kelsey	University: Striving Research 3	Associate vice president, Articulation	F	Administrator	1	Incumbent
Community college staff						
Val	Community College: CCC	Vice president, Student Services	F	Administrator	17	Challenger
Mark	Community College: CCC	Specialist, Transfer Advising	M	Advisor	11	Implementer
Sofia	Community College: CCC	Coordinator, Transfer Resources	F	Administrator	10	Implementer
Nina	Community College: CCC	Specialist, Transfer Student Services	F	Advisor	6	Challenger
Alicia	Community College: CCC	Advising specialist	F	Advisor	8	Implementer
Tim	Community College: CCC	Advisor, supervisor	M	Advising leader	10	Implementer

(*continued*)

Table A.2. Description of featured staff interviewees (continued)

Pseudonym	Campus type	Title	Gender	Job description	Years in role	Role in the field
Dennis	Community College: CCC	Advisor, supervisor	M	Advising leader	3	Implementer
Camila	Community College: FCCS	Advisor, team leader	F	Advising leader	10	Implementer
Andrea	Community College: FCCS/University Rep	Advisor, team leader	F	Advising leader	1	Implementer
Celeste	Community College: FCCS	Advisor, team lead	F	Advising leader	3	Implementer
Rick	Community College: FCCS	Vice president, Student Success	F	Administrator	5	Challenger
Lloyd	Community College: FCCS	Professor and advisor	M	Advisor	N/A	Challenger

Note: This table presents descriptive information for staff described in chapter 2 (university personnel) and chapter 3 (community college personnel).

NOTES

FOREWORD

1. Burton R. Clark, *The Open Door College: A Case Study* (New York: McGraw-Hill, 1960); Jerome Karabel, "Community Colleges and Social Stratification," *Harvard Educational Review* 42, no. 4 (1972): 521–62; Jerome Karabel, "Protecting the Portals: Class and the Community College," *Social Policy* 5, no. 1 (1974): 12–19.
2. Steven Brint and Jerome Karabel, *The Diverted Dream: Community Colleges and the Promise of Educational Opportunity in America, 1900–1985* (New York: Oxford University Press, 1989); Steven Brint and Jerome Karabel, "Institutional Origins and Transformations: The Case of American Community Colleges," in *The New Institutionalism in Organizational Analysis*, edited by Walter W. Powell and Paul J. DiMaggio (Chicago: University of Chicago Press, 1991); Clark, *Open Door College*; Kevin J. Dougherty, *The Contradictory College: The Conflicting Origins, Impacts, and Futures of the Community College* (Albany: State University of New York, 1994); Kevin J. Dougherty, "The Evolving Role of the Community College: Policy Issues and Research Questions," in *Higher Education: Handbook of Theory and Research*, vol. 17, edited by John C. Smart and William G. Tierney (New York: Kluwer, 2002).
3. Brint and Karabel, *Diverted Dream;* Brint and Karabel, "Institutional Origins and Transformations"; Dougherty, *Contradictory College*; Dougherty, "Evolving Role."

4. Neil Fligstein and Doug McAdam, *A Theory of Fields* (New York: Oxford University Press, 2012).
5. Thomas Bailey, Shanna Smith Jaggars, and Davis Jenkins, *Redesigning America's Community Colleges: A Clearer Path to Success* (Cambridge, MA: Harvard University Press, 2015); Kevin J. Dougherty, *Choice Is Not Always Good: Reducing the Role of Informational Inequality in Producing and Legitimating Higher Education Inequality* (New York: Columbia University, Teachers College, Community College Research Center, 2023), https://ccrc.tc.columbia.edu/publications/choice-is-not-always-good.html; James E. Rosenbaum, Regina Deil-Amen, and Ann E. Person, *After Admission: From College Access to College Success* (New York: Russell Sage Foundation, 2006).

INTRODUCTION

1. Doug Shapiro, Afet Dundar, Faye Huie, Phoebe Khasiala Wakhungu, Xin Yuan, Angel Nathan, and Youngsik Hwang, *Tracking Transfer: Measures of Effectiveness in Helping Community College Students to Complete Bachelor's Degrees* (Herndon, VA: National Student Clearinghouse, September 2017), https://files.eric.ed.gov/fulltext/ED580214.pdf.
2. Shapiro et al., *Tracking Transfer.*
3. Xueli Wang, *On My Own: The Challenge and Promise of Building Equitable STEM Transfer Pathways* (Cambridge, MA: Harvard Education Press, 2021), 87.
4. Steven G. Brint and Jerome Karabel, *The Diverted Dream: Community Colleges and the Promise of Educational Opportunity in America, 1900–1985* (New York: Oxford University Press on Demand, 1989); Burton R. Clark, "The 'Cooling-Out' Function in Higher Education," *American Journal of Sociology* 65, no. 6 (1960): 569–76, https://doi.org/10.1086/222787.
5. Thomas R. Bailey, Shanna S. Jaggars, and Davis Jenkins, *Redesigning America's Community Colleges: A Clearer Path to Student Success* (Cambridge, MA: Harvard University Press, 2015); James E. Rosenbaum, Regina Deil-Amen, and Ann E. Person, *After Admission: From College Access to College Success* (New York: Russell Sage Foundation, 2007); Judith Scott-Clayton, "The Shapeless River: Does a Lack of Structure Inhibit Students'

Progress at Community Colleges?" (CCRC working paper no. 25, New York: Columbia University, 2011), https://files.eric.ed.gov/fulltext/ED515131.pdf.

6. Percentage of students educated by Texas community colleges calculated by authors using Integrated Postsecondary Education Data System (IPEDS) data. Texas Higher Education Coordinating Board [THECB], *Texas General Academic Institutions: Increasing Successful Community College Transfer* (Austin, TX: THECB, 2014), http://www.thecb.state.tx.us/DocID/pdf/6073.pdf.
7. Robert O. Berdahl, *Statewide Coordination of Higher Education* (Washington, DC: American Council on Education, 1971).
8. We use the terms "two-year" and "four-year" at times to differentiate between community colleges and baccalaureate-granting universities, as is common in public and policy discussions, though we acknowledge many students do not transfer or complete associate degrees within two years and that many students take longer than four years to complete a bachelor's degree (and that some community colleges have also started to offer bachelor's degrees). We also refer to four-year institutions as "universities" throughout the book, which is prevalent terminology in the Texas context where our data was collected.
9. David B. Monaghan and Paul Attewell, "The Community College Route to the Bachelor's Degree," *Educational Evaluation and Policy Analysis* 37, no. 1 (2015): 70–91, https://doi.org/10.3102/0162373714521865; Lauren Schudde and Raymond Stanley Brown, "Understanding Variation in Estimates of Diversionary Effects of Community College Entrance: A Systematic Review and Meta-Analysis," *Sociology of Education* 92, no. 3 (2019): 247–68, https://doi.org/10.1177%2F0038040719848445.
10. Thomas Bailey, Paul Davis Jenkins, John Fink, Jenna Cullinane, and Lauren Schudde, *Policy Levers to Strengthen Community College Transfer Student Success in Texas* (New York: Columbia University, 2016), https://doi.org/10.7916/D8JS9W20; Davis Jenkins and John Fink, *Tracking Transfer: New Measures of Institutional and State Effectiveness in Helping Community*

College Students Attain Bachelor's Degrees (New York: Columbia University, 2016), https://doi.org/10.7916/D8C24W80.

11. Bailey, Jaggars, and Jenkins, *Redesigning America's Community Colleges*; Bailey et al., *Policy Levers*; Michelle Hodara, Mary Martinez-Wenzl, David Stevens, and Christopher Mazzeo, "Exploring Credit Mobility and Major-Specific Pathways: A Policy Analysis and Student Perspective on Community College to University Transfer," *Community College Review* 45, no. 4 (2017): 331–49, https://doi.org/10.1177/0091552117724197.
12. Jason L. Taylor and Dimpal Jain, "The Multiple Dimensions of Transfer: Examining the Transfer Function in American Higher Education," *Community College Review* 45, no. 4 (2017): 273–93, https://doi.org/10.1177%2F0091552117725177; Jason L. Taylor, "Reverse Credit Transfer Policies and Programs: Policy Rationales, Implementation, and Implications," *Community College Journal of Research and Practice* 40, no. 12 (2016): 1074–90, https://doi.org/10.1080/10668926.2016.1213673.
13. Alexander C. McCormick, "Swirling and Double-Dipping: New Patterns of Student Attendance and Their Implications for Higher Education," *New Directions for Higher Education*, 2003: 13–24, https://doi-org.ezproxy.lib.utexas.edu/10.1002/he.98.
14. Cassidy Francies and Lexi Anderson, *50-State Comparison: Transfer and Articulation Policies* (Denver: Education Commission of the States, 2020), https://www.ecs.org/transfer-and-articulation-policies-db/.
15. Angela Boatman and Adela Soliz, "Statewide Transfer Policies and Community College Student Success," *Education Finance and Policy 13*, no. 4 (2018): 449–83. https://doi.org/10.1162/edfp_a_00233; Lauren Schudde, Ibrahim Bicak, and Meghan Shea, "Getting to the Core of Credit Transfer: How Do Pre-Transfer Core Credits Predict Baccalaureate Attainment for Community College Transfer Students?," *Educational Policy* 37, no. 4 (2023): 1014–43, https://doi.org/10.1177%2F08959048211049415; George Spencer, "Can Transfer Guides Improve the Uptake of Major Prerequisites? Evidence from Ohio's Transfer and Articulation Policy Reform,"

Research in Higher Education 60, no. 4 (2019): 458–84, https://doi.org/10.1007/s11162-018-9522-2.

16. Hodara et al., "Exploring Credit Mobility."
17. Josipa Roksa and Bruce Keith, "Credits, Time, and Attainment: Articulation Policies and Success After Transfer," *Educational Evaluation and Policy Analysis* 30, no. 3 (2008): 236–54, https://doi.org/10.3102/0162373708321383.
18. Francies and Anderson, *50-State Comparison*; Megan Root, *Essential Elements of State Policy for College Completion: Statewide Transfer Policies* (Atlanta: Southern Regional Education Board, 2013), https://www.sreb.org/sites/main/files/file-attachments/013_ess_elem_state_tran.pdf.
19. John Fink and Davis Jenkins, "Takes Two to Tango: Essential Practices of Highly Effective Transfer Partnerships," *Community College Review* 45, no. 4 (2017): 294–310, https://doi.org/10.1177/0091552117724512.
20. Root, *Essential Elements*; Lauren Schudde, Huriya Jabbar, Eliza Epstein, and Elif Yucel, "Students' Sense Making of Higher Education Policies During the Vertical Transfer Process," *American Educational Research Journal* 58, no. 5 (2021): 921–53, https://doi.org/10.3102%2F00028312211003050.
21. Francies and Anderson, *50-State Comparison.*
22. Jason L. Taylor and Matthew Giani, "Modeling the Effect of the Reverse Credit Transfer Associate's Degree: Evidence from Two States," *Review of Higher Education* 42, no. 2 (2019): 427–55, https://doi.org/10.1353/rhe.2019.0002.
23. Francies and Anderson, *50-State Comparison.*
24. Bailey et al., *Policy Levers.*
25. Hodara et al., "Exploring Credit Mobility"; Schudde et al., "Students' Sense Making."
26. Erin Dunlop Velez et al., "Baccalaureate and Beyond (B&B:16/17): A First Look at the Employment and Educational Experiences of College Graduates, 1 Year Later" (Washington, DC: National Center for Education Statistics, 2019), Table 2, https://nces.ed.gov/fastfacts/display.asp?id=569.
27. America Counts staff, "Texas Added Almost 4 Million People in Last Decade," *Texas: 2020 Census*, August 25, 2021,

https://www.census.gov/library/stories/state-by-state/texas-population-change-between-census-decade.html.

28. America Counts staff, 2021, "Texas Added Almost 4 Million People in Last Decade."
29. Laura W. Perna and Joni E. Finney, *The Attainment Agenda: State Policy Leadership in Higher Education* (Baltimore: Johns Hopkins University Press, 2014); Texas Higher Education Coordinating Board, *Texas Public Higher Education Almanac: A Profile of State and Institutional Performance and Characteristics* (Austin, TX: THECB, Summer 2021), https://reportcenter.highered.texas.gov/agency-publication/almanac/2021-texas-public-higher-education-almanac/.
30. Berdahl, *Statewide Coordination of Higher Education.*
31. Robert O. Berdahl, "Universities and Governments in the 21st Century: The US Experience," in *Towards a New Model of Governance for Universities? A Comparative View*, edited by Dietmar Braun and Francois-Xavier Merrien (Philadelphia: J. Kingsley, 1999), 53:59–77; Lauren Schudde, Huriya Jabbar, and Catherine Hartman, "How Political and Ecological Contexts Shape Community College Transfer," *Sociology of Education* 94, no. 1 (2021): 65–83, https://doi.org/10.1177/0038040720954817.
32. Perna and Finney, *Attainment Agenda.*
33. Michelle Hodara, Mary Martinez-Wenzl, David Stevens, Christopher Mazzeo, *Improving Credit Mobility for Community College Transfer Students* (Portland, OR: Education Northwest, 2016), https://www.luminafoundation.org/wp-content/uploads/2017/08/improving-credit-mobility.pdf; Hodara et al., "Exploring Credit Mobility."
34. THECB, *Improving Transfer to Increase Student Success* (Austin: Texas Higher Education Coordinating Board, 2014); Texas Higher Education Coordinating Board, *Update on Implementation of SB25 and a Progress Summary of the Improving Transfer in Texas Working Group* (Austin, TX: THECB, 2021), https://reportcenter.highered.texas.gov/meeting/board-supporting-documents/january-board-2021-update-on-texas-transfer-framework-ppt/.

35. Hodara et al., *Improving Credit Mobility*.
36. Fink and Jenkins, "Takes Two"; Hodara et al., *Improving Credit Mobility*.
37. Fink and Jenkins, "Takes Two"; Stephen J. Handel and Ronald A. Williams, *The Promise of the Transfer Pathway: Opportunity and Challenge for Community College Students Seeking the Baccalaureate Degree* (New York: College Board, 2012), https://files.eric.ed.gov/fulltext/ED541978.pdf.
38. Bailey et al., *Policy Levers*.
39. Linda S. Hagedorn, "The Pursuit of Student Success: The Directions and Challenges Facing Community Colleges," in *Higher Education: Handbook of Theory and Research*, edited by Michael B. Paulsen (New York: Springer, 2010), 25: 181–218; Barbara K. Townsend and Kristin Wilson, "'A Hand Hold for a Little Bit': Factors Facilitating the Success of Community College Transfer Students to a Large Research University," *Journal of College Student Development* 47, no. 4 (2006): 439–56, https://doi.org/10.1353/csd.2006.0052.
40. Schudde et al., "Students' Sense Making."
41. Janine M. Allen, Cathleen L. Smith, and Jeanette K. Muehleck, "Pre- and Post-Transfer Academic Advising: What Students Say Are the Similarities and Differences," *Journal of College Student Development* 55, no. 4 (2014): 353–67, https://doi.org/10.1353/csd.2014.0034; Government Accountability Office (GAO), *Students Need More Information to Help Reduce Challenges Transferring Credits* (Washington, DC: U.S. Government Printing Office, 2017); Alfred Herrera and Dimpal Jain, "Building a Transfer-Receptive Culture at Four-Year Institutions," *New Directions for Higher Education* 2013, no. 162 (2013): 51–59, https://doi.org/10.1002/he.20056; Dimpal Jain, Alfred Herrera, Santiago Bernal, and Daniel Solorzano, "Critical Race Theory and the Transfer Function: Introducing a Transfer Receptive Culture," *Community College Journal of Research and Practice* 35, no. 3 (2011): 252–66, https://doi.org/10.1080/10668926.2011.526525.
42. GAO, *Students Need More*; Lauren Schudde, Dwuana Bradley, and Caitlin Absher, "Navigating Vertical Transfer Online:

Access to and Usefulness of Transfer Information on Community College Websites," *Community College Review* 48, no. 1 (2020): 3–30, https://doi.org/10.1177/0091552119874500.

43. Monaghan and Attewell, "Community College Route"; Di Xu, Shanna Smith Jaggars, Jeffrey Fletcher, and John Fink, "Are Community College Transfer Students 'a Good Bet' for 4-Year Admissions? Comparing Academic and Labor-Market Outcomes Between Transfer and Native 4-Year College Students," *Journal of Higher Education* 89, no. 4 (2018): 478–502, https://doi.org/10.1080/00221546.2018.1434280.
44. Miriam J. Metzger, Andrew J. Flanagin, and Lara Zwarun, "College Student Web Use, Perceptions of Information Credibility, and Verification Behavior," *Computers & Education* 41, no. 3 (2003): 271–90, 281, https://doi.org/10.1016/S0360-1315(03)00049-6; Elif Yücel, Huriya Jabbar, and Lauren Schudde, "Navigating Transfer Through Networks: How Community College Students Seek Support From Social Ties Throughout the Transfer Process," *Review of Higher Education* 45, no. 4 (2022), 487–513, http://doi.org/10.1353/rhe.2022.0006.
45. James S. Coleman, "Social Capital in the Creation of Human Capital," *American Journal of Sociology* 94 (1988): S95–S120, S104, https://doi.org/10.1086/228943; Regina Deil-Amen and James E. Rosenbaum, "The Social Prerequisites of Success: Can College Structure Reduce the Need for Social Know-How?" *Annals of the American Academy of Political and Social Science* 580 (2003): 120–43, https://doi.org/10.1177/0002716202250216.
46. Alexandra W. Logue, *Pathways to Reform: Credits and Conflict at the City University of New York* (Princeton, NJ: Princeton University Press, 2017); Perna and Finney, *Attainment Agenda.*
47. Kevin Dougherty, *The Contradictory College: The Conflicting Origins, Impacts, and Futures of the Community College* (Albany: SUNY Press, 1994).
48. Bailey et al., *Policy Levers*; Logue, *Pathways to Reform*; Perna and Finney, *Attainment Agenda.*
49. Alicia C. Dowd, "Improving Transfer Access for Low-Income Community College Students," in *Recognizing and Serving*

Low-Income Students in Postsecondary Education: An Examination of Institutional Policies, Practices, and Culture, edited by Adrianna Kezar (New York: Routledge, 2010), 217–31.

50. Texas Higher Education Coordinating Board, "Institutional Resumes" (Austin, TX: THECB, 2017), http://www.thecb.state.tx.us/apps/resumes/.
51. Texas Higher Education Board, "Institutional Resumes."
52. Neil Fligstein and Doug McAdam, "Toward a General Theory of Strategic Action Fields," *Sociological Theory* 29, no. 1 (2011): 1–26, https://doi.org/10.1111/j.1467-9558.2010.01385.x.

CHAPTER I

1. Steven G. Brint and Jerome Karabel, *The Diverted Dream: Community Colleges and the Promise of Educational Opportunity in America, 1900–1985* (New York: Oxford University Press on Demand, 1989); Arturo Gonzalez and Michael J. Hilmer, "The Role of 2-Year Colleges in the Improving Situation of Hispanic Postsecondary Education," *Economics of Education Review* 25, no. 3 (2006): 249–57, https://doi.org/10.1016/j.econedurev.2004.12.002; Duane E. Leigh and Andrew M. Gill, "Do Community Colleges Really Divert Students from Earning Bachelor's Degrees?," *Economics of Education Review* 22, no. 1 (2003): 23–30, https://doi.org/10.1016/S0272-7757(01)00057-7; Cecilia Elena Rouse, "Democratization or Diversion? The Effect of Community Colleges on Educational Attainment," *Journal of Business & Economic Statistics* 13, no. 2 (1995): 217–24, https://doi.org/10.1080/07350015.1995.10524596.
2. Brint and Karabel, *Diverted Dream*; Steven Brint, Mark Riddle, and Robert A. Hanneman, "Reference Sets, Identities, and Aspirations in a Complex Organizational Field: The Case of American Four-Year Colleges and Universities," *Sociology of Education* 79, no. 3 (2006): 229–52, https://doi.org/10.1177/003804070607900303; Bridget Terry Long and Michal Kurlaender, "Do Community Colleges Provide a Viable Pathway to a Baccalaureate Degree?," *Educational Evaluation and Policy Analysis* 31, no. 1 (2009): 30–53; Judith Scott-Clayton, "The Shapeless River: Does a Lack of Structure Inhibit Students'

Progress at Community College?" (CCRC working paper no. 25, New York: Columbia University, 2011), https://files.eric.ed.gov/fulltext/ED515131.pdf.

3. Lauren Schudde and Raymond Stanley Brown, "Understanding Variation in Estimates of Diversionary Effects of Community College Entrance: A Systematic Review and Meta-Analysis," *Sociology of Education* 92, no. 3 (July 2019): 247–68, https://doi.org/10.1177/0038040719848445.
4. Kevin Dougherty, *The Contradictory College: The Conflicting Origins, Impacts, and Futures of the Community College* (Albany: SUNY Press, 1994); Debra Bragg, Theresa Ling Yeh, Lia Wetzstein, and Elizabeth Apple Meza, eds., "Transfer Partnerships for Improved Equity and Outcomes," *New Directions for Community Colleges* 2020, no. 192 (August 2020): 1–124; Jennie Brand, Fabian Pfeffer, and Sara Goldrick-Rab, "The Community College Effect Revisited: The Importance of Attending to Heterogeneity and Complex Counterfactuals," *Sociological Science*, 1 (October 2014): 448–65, https://doi.org/10.15195/v1.a25; Jack Mountjoy, "Community Colleges and Upward Mobility," *American Economic Review*, 112, no. 8 (2022), 2580–630, https://doi.org/10.1257/aer.20181756.
5. Burton Clark, *The Open Door College: A Case Study* (New York: McGraw-Hill, 1960); Burton Clark, "The Cooling-Out Function in Higher Education," *American Journal of Sociology* 65, no. 6 (1960): 569–76, https://www.jstor.org/stable/2773649; Brint and Karabel, *Diverted Dream*, 7–10; Dougherty, *Contradictory College*.
6. Gloria Crisp and Anne-Marie Nuñez, "Understanding the Racial Transfer Gap: Modeling Underrepresented Minority and Nonminority Students' Pathways from Two-to Four-Year Institutions," *Review of Higher Education* 37, no. 3 (2014): 291–320, https://doi.org/10.1353/rhe.2014.0017; William R. Doyle, "Impact of Increased Academic Intensity on Transfer Rates: An Application of Matching Estimators to Student-Unit Record Data," *Research in Higher Education* 50, no. 1 (2009): 52–72, https://doi.org/10.1007/s11162-008-9107-6; Kathleen M. Shaw and Howard B. London, "Culture and Ideology in Keeping Transfer Commitment: Three Community

Colleges," *Review of Higher Education* 25, no. 1 (2001): 91–114, https://doi.org/10.1353/rhe.2001.0015; Robert Wassmer, Colleen Moore, and Nancy Shulock, "Effect of Racial/Ethnic Composition on Transfer Rates in Community Colleges: Implications for Policy and Practice," *Research in Higher Education* 45, no. 6 (2004): 651–72, https://doi.org/10.1023/B:RIHE.0000040267.68949.d1.

7. Clark, *Open Door College*; Clark, "Cooling-Out Function," 574.
8. Brint and Karabel, *Diverted Dream*, 7–10.
9. James E. Rosenbaum, Regina Deil-Amen, and Ann E. Person, *After Admission: From College Access to College Success* (New York: Russell Sage Foundation, 2007); Schudde and Brown, "Understanding Variation."
10. Wassmer, Moore, and Shulock, "Effect of Racial/Ethnic Composition"; Crisp and Nuñez, "Understanding the Racial Transfer Gap."
11. Crisp and Nuñez, "Understanding the Racial Transfer Gap."
12. Karl Alexander, Robert Bozick, and Doris Entwisle, "Warming Up, Cooling Out, or Holding Steady? Persistence and Change in Educational Expectations After High School," *Sociology of Education* 81, no. 4 (2008): 371–96, https://doi.org/10.1177/003804070808100403; Kelly Nielsen, "'Fake It 'til You Make It': Why Community College Students' Aspirations 'Hold Steady,'" *Sociology of Education* 88, no. 4 (2015): 265–83, https://doi.org/10.1177/0038040715601889.
13. Thomas R. Bailey, Shanna S. Jaggars, and Davis Jenkins, *Redesigning America's Community Colleges: A Clearer Path to Student Success* (Cambridge, MA: Harvard University Press, 2015); Rosenbaum, Deil-Amen, and Person, *After Admission*; Scott-Clayton, "Shapeless River."
14. Bailey, Jaggars, and Jenkins, *Redesigning America's Community Colleges*; John Fink and Davis Jenkins, "Takes Two to Tango: Essential Practices of Highly Effective Transfer Partnerships," *Community College Review* 45, no. 4 (2017): 294–310, https://doi.org/10.1177/0091552117724512; Rosenbaum, Deil-Amen, and Person, *After Admission*; Scott-Clayton, "Shapeless River"; Lauren Schudde, Dwuana Bradley, and Caitlin Absher, "Navigating Vertical Transfer Online: Access

to and Usefulness of Transfer Information on Community College Websites," *Community College Review* 48, no. 1 (2020): 3–30, https://doi.org/10.1177/0091552119874500.

15. Janine M. Allen, Cathleen L. Smith, and Jeanette K. Muehleck, "Pre- and Post-Transfer Academic Advising: What Students Say Are the Similarities and Differences," *Journal of College Student Development* 55, no. 4 (2014): 353–67, https://doi.org/10.1353/csd.2014.0034; Rosenbaum, Deil-Amen, and Person, *After Admission*, 63.
16. Janine M. Allen, Cathleen L. Smith, and Jeanette K. Muehleck, "Pre- and Post-Transfer Academic Advising"; Timothy G. Davies and Ellyn M. Dickmann, "Student Voices in the Transfer Process: Do We Hear Them? Do We Listen?," *Community College Journal of Research and Practice* 22, no. 5 (1998): 541–57, https://doi.org/10.1080/1066892980220507; Government Accountability Office [GAO], *Students Need More Information to Help Reduce Challenges Transferring Credits* (Washington, DC: U.S. Government Printing Office, 2017); Alfred Herrera and Dimpal Jain, "Building a Transfer-Receptive Culture at Four-Year Institutions," *New Directions for Higher Education* 2013, no. 162 (2013): 51–59, https://doi.org/10.1002/he.20056; Dimpal Jain, Alfred Herrera, Santiago Bernal, and Daniel Solorzano, "Critical Race Theory and the Transfer Function: Introducing a Transfer Receptive Culture," *Community College Journal of Research and Practice* 35, no. 3 (2011): 252–66, https://doi.org/10.1080/10668926.2011.526525; Kathryn C. Senie, "Implementing Transfer and Articulation: A Case Study of Community Colleges and State Universities," *Community College Journal of Research and Practice* 40, no. 4 (2016): 269–84, https://doi.org/10.1080/10668926.2015.1038667.
17. Scott-Clayton, "Shapeless River."
18. Xueli Wang, *On My Own: The Challenge and Promise of Building Equitable STEM Transfer Pathways* (Cambridge, MA: Harvard Education Press, 2020), 146–47.
19. Wang, *On My Own*, 146.
20. Patricia M. McDonough, *Choosing Colleges: How Social Class and Schools Structure Opportunity* (Albany: State University of New York Press, 1997); Laura W. Perna, "Understanding the

Relationship Between Information About College Prices and Financial Aid and Students' College-Related Behaviors," *The American Behavioral Scientist* 49, no. 12 (2006): 1620–35, https://doi.org/10.1177/0002764206289144; Rosenbaum, Deil-Amen, and Person, *After Admission*; Elif Yücel, Huriya Jabbar, and Lauren Schudde, "Navigating Transfer Through Networks: How Community College Students Seek Support From Social Ties Throughout the Transfer Process," *Review of Higher Education* 45, no. 4 (2022): 487–513, http://doi.org/10.1353/rhe.2022.0006.

21. Tara Yosso, "Whose Culture Has Capital? A Critical Race Theory Discussion of Community Cultural Wealth," *Race, Ethnicity, and Education* 8, no. 1 (2005): 69–91; Rosenbaum, Deil-Amen, and Person, *After Admission*, 63.
22. Susan Choy, "Nontraditional Undergraduates: Findings from the Condition of Education 2002" (Washington, DC: National Center for Education Statistics, August 2002), https://nces.ed.gov/pubs2002/2002012.pdf.
23. Regina Deil-Amen and James E. Rosenbaum, "The Social Prerequisites of Success: Can College Structure Reduce the Need for Social Know-How?," *Annals of the American Academy of Political and Social Science* 586 (2003): 120–43, https://doi.org/10.1177/0002716202250216.
24. Allen, Smith, and Muehleck, "Pre- and Post-Transfer Academic Advising"; Davies and Dickmann, "Student Voices"; Lauren Schudde, Catilin Absher, and Dwuana Bradley, "Ease of Access and Usefulness of Transfer Information on Community College Websites in Texas," Community College Research Center Working Paper no. 102 (2018).
25. Allen, Smith, and Muehleck, "Pre- and Post-Transfer Academic Advising;" Rosenbaum, Deil-Amen, and Person, *After Admission*, 63.
26. Allen, Smith, and Muehleck, "Pre- and Post-Transfer Academic Advising;" Rosenbaum, Deil-Amen, and Person, *After Admission*, 63; Deil-Amen and Rosenbaum, "Social Prerequisites of Success," 120–43.
27. Lauren Schudde, Huriya Jabbar, Eliza Epstein, and Elif Yucel, "Students' Sense Making of Higher Education Policies

During the Vertical Transfer Process," *American Educational Research Journal* 58, no. 5 (October 2021): 921–53, https://doi.org/10.3102/00028312211003050; Schudde, Bradley, and Absher, "Navigating Vertical Transfer Online," 3–30.

28. Huriya Jabbar, Carmen Serrata, Eliza Epstein, and Joanna Sánchez, "'Échale Ganas': Family Support of Latino/a Community College Students' Transfer to Four-Year Universities," *Journal of Latinos and Education* 18, no. 3 (2019): 258–76, https://doi:10.1080/15348431.2017.1390462; Lauren Schudde, Huriya Jabbar, and Catherine Hartman, "How Political and Ecological Contexts Shape Community College Transfer," *Sociology of Education* 94, no. 1 (2021): 65–83, https://doi.org/10.1177/0038040720954817; Miriam J. Metzger, Andrew J. Flanagin, and Lara Zwarun, "College Student Web Use, Perceptions of Information Credibility, and Verification Behavior," *Computers & Education* 41, no. 3 (2003): 271–90, 281, https://doi.org/10.1016/S0360-1315(03)00049-6.
29. Scott-Clayton, "Shapeless River."
30. Eric P. Bettinger and Rachel B. Baker, "The Effects of Student Coaching: An Evaluation of a Randomized Experiment in Student Advising," *Educational Evaluation and Policy Analysis* 36, no. 1 (2014): 3–19; GAO, *Students Need More Information.*
31. Thomas R. Bailey, Davis Jenkins, John Fink, Jenna Cullinane, and Lauren Schudde, *Policy Levers to Strengthen Community College Transfer Student Success in Texas: Report to the Greater Texas Foundation* (New York: Teachers College, Columbia University, 2016); Michelle Hodara, Mary Martinez-Wenzl, David Stevens, and Christopher Mazzeo, "Exploring Credit Mobility and Major-Specific Pathways: A Policy Analysis and Student Perspective on Community College to University Transfer," *Community College Review* 45, no. 4 (2017): 331–49, https://doi.org/10.1177/0091552117724197.
32. Linda Serra Hagedorn, "The Pursuit of Student Success: The Directions and Challenges Facing Community Colleges," in *Higher Education: Handbook of Theory and Research,* edited by J. C. Smart (New York: Springer, 2019), 4:181–218; Barbara K. Townsend and Kristin Wilson, "'A Hand Hold for A Little Bit': Factors Facilitating the Success of Community College

Transfer Students to a Large Research University," *Journal of College Student Development* 47, no. 4 (2006): 439–56, https://doi.org/10.1353/csd.2006.0052.

33. Allen, Smith, and Muehleck, "Pre- and Post-Transfer Academic Advising"; Peter Riley Bahr, "Cooling Out in the Community College: What Is the Effect of Academic Advising on Students' Chances of Success?," *Research in Higher Education* 49, no. 8 (2008): 704–32, https://doi.org/10.1007/s11162-008-9100-0; Davies and Dickmann, "Student Voices."
34. Schudde, Bradley, and Absher, "Navigating Vertical Transfer Online;" GAO, *Students Need More Information.*
35. GAO, *Students Need More Information.*
36. Schudde et al., "Students' Sense Making."
37. Robin LaSota and William Zumeta, "What Matters in Increasing Community College Students' Upward Transfer to the Baccalaureate Degree: Findings from the Beginning Postsecondary Study 2003–2009," *Research In Higher Education*, 57, no. 2 (2016): 152–89, https://doi.org/10.1007/s11162-015-9381-z; Josipa Roksa and Bruce Keith, "Credits, Time, and Attainment: Articulation Policies and Success After Transfer," *Educational Evaluation and Policy Analysis*, 30, no. 3 (2008): 236–54, https://doi.org/10.3102/0162373708321383.
38. Bailey, Jaggars, and Jenkins, *Redesigning America's Community Colleges*; Bailey et al., *Policy Levers*; Alicia C. Dowd, "Improving Transfer Access for Low-Income Community College Students," in *Recognizing and Serving Low-Income Students in Postsecondary Education: An Examination of Institutional Policies, Practices, and Culture*, edited by Adrianna Kezar (New York: Routledge, 2010), 217–31; Hodara et al., "Exploring Credit Mobility," 331–49.
39. Ann E. Person, James E. Rosenbaum, and Regina Deil-Amen, "Student Planning and Information Problems in Different College Structures," *Teachers College Record* 108, no. 103 (March 2006): 374–96, https://coe.arizona.edu/sites/default/files/migrated/StudentPlanningandInfoProblems.TCR.pdf.
40. Huriya Jabbar et al., "Thinking Through Transfer: Examining How Community College Students Make Transfer Decisions," *Community College Review* 49, no. 1 (January 2021):

3–29, https://doi.org/10.1177/0091552120964876; Schudde et al., "Students' Sense Making."

41. Herrera and Jain, "Building a Transfer-Receptive Culture"; Alicia C. Dowd, John J. Cheslock, and Tatiana Melguizo, "Transfer Access from Community Colleges and the Distribution of Elite Higher Education," *Journal of Higher Education* 79, no. 4 (2008), 442–72, https://doi.org/10.1353/jhe.0.0010.
42. Jain et al., "Critical Race Theory"; Dimpal Jain, Santiago Bernal, Iris Lucero, Alfred Herrera, and Daniel Solorzano, "Toward a Critical Race Perspective of Transfer: An Exploration of Transfer Receptive Culture," *Community College Journal of Research and Practice* 40, no. 12 (2016): 1013–24.
43. Daniel Klasik, "The College Application Gauntlet: A Systematic Analysis of the Steps to Four-Year College Enrollment," *Research in Higher Education* 53, no. 5 (2012): 506–49, https://doi.org/10.1007/s11162-011-9242-3; Annette Lareau and Elliot B. Weininger, "Class and the Transition to Adulthood," in *Social Class: How Does It Work?*, edited by Annette Lareau and Dalton Conley (New York: Russell Sage Foundation, 2008), 118–51.
44. Jabbar et al., "Thinking Through Transfer."
45. David S. Yeager et al., "Teaching a Lay Theory Before College Narrows Achievement Gaps at Scale," *Proceedings of the National Academy of Sciences—PNAS* 113, no. 24 (June 14, 2016): E3341–48, https://doi.org/10.1073/pnas.152436011.
46. Alexandra W. Logue, *Pathways to Reform: Credits and Conflict at the City University of New York* (Princeton, NJ: Princeton University Press, 2017); Laura W. Perna and Joni E. Finney, *The Attainment Agenda: State Policy Leadership in Higher Education* (Baltimore: Johns Hopkins University Press, 2014).
47. Hodara et al., "Exploring Credit Mobility"; Herrera and Jain, "Building a Transfer-Receptive Culture"; Logue, *Pathways to Reform*; GAO, *Students Need More Information*, 13.
48. Bailey et al., *Policy Levers*; Logue, *Pathways to Reform*; Perna and Finney, *Attainment Agenda*.
49. Sonya Joseph and Mark Allen Poisel, eds., *Building Transfer Student Pathways for College and Career Success* (Columbia, NC:

National Resource Center for The First-Year Experience and Students in Transition, 2018).

50. John W. Meyer and Brian Rowan, "Institutionalized Organizations: Formal Structure as Myth and Ceremony," *American Journal of Sociology* 83, no. 2 (1977): 340–63, https://www.jstor.org/stable/2778293.
51. Dougherty, *Contradictory College*; David F. Labaree, "Public Goods, Private Goods: The American Struggle over Educational Goals," *American Educational Research Journal* 34, no. 1 (1997): 39–82, https://doi.org/10.3102/00028312034001039.
52. Adam Gamoran and Robert Dreeben, "Coupling and Control in Educational Organizations," *Administrative Science Quarterly* 31, no. 4 (1986): 612–32, https://doi.org/10.2307/2392966; Talcott Parsons, *Structure and Process in Modern Societies* (Glencoe, IL: Free Press, 1960).
53. Paul J. DiMaggio and Walter W. Powell, "The Iron Cage Revisited: Institutional Isomorphism and Collective Rationality in Organizational Fields," *American Sociological Review* 48, no. 2 (1983): 147–60, https://doi.org/10.2307/2095101.
54. Neil Fligstein and Doug McAdam, "Toward a General Theory of Strategic Action Fields," *Sociological Theory* 29, no. 1 (2011): 1–26, https://doi.org/10.1111/j.1467-9558.2010.01385.x; Neil Fligstein and Doug McAdam, *A Theory of Fields* (Oxford University Press, 2012).
55. Fligstein and McAdam, "Toward a General Theory," 3.
56. Fligstein and McAdam, "Toward a General Theory," 4.
57. Fligstein and McAdam, "Toward a General Theory," 5.
58. Fligstein and McAdam, "Toward a General Theory," 5.
59. Fligstein and McAdam, "Toward a General Theory," 6; Jack Goldstone and Bert Useem, "Putting Values and Institutions Back into the Theory of Strategic Action Fields," *Sociological Theory* 30, no. 1 (2012): 37–47.
60. Fligstein and McAdam, "Toward a General Theory," 6.
61. Schudde, Jabbar, and Hartman, "How Political and Ecological Contexts."
62. Fligstein and McAdam, "Toward a General Theory," 1–26.
63. Fligstein and McAdam, *Theory of Fields*, 12.

64. Schudde, Jabbar, and Hartman, "How Political and Ecological Contexts."
65. Bailey et al., *Policy Levers*.
66. Lauren Schudde, Huriya Jabbar, and Andrea Chevalier, "To Improve Community College Transfer in Texas, Students Need Better Information" (policy brief, Austin: Population Research Center, University of Texas at Austin, 2018), https://repositories.lib.utexas.edu/bitstream/handle/2152/71426/prc-brief-3-17-schudde-tx-transfer-project.pdf.

CHAPTER 2

1. University of Texas at Austin, *2020–2021 Stat Handbook* (Austin: The University of Texas at Austin Institutional Reporting, Research, and Information Systems, 2021).
2. Texas Higher Education Coordinating Board, "Texas Core Curriculum" (Austin, TX: THECB, 2018), https://reportcenter.highered.texas.gov/agency-publication/miscellaneous/elements-of-the-texas-core-curriculum/.
3. Lauren Schudde, Catilin Absher, and Dwuana Bradley, "Ease of Access and Usefulness of Transfer Information on Community College Websites in Texas," Community College Research Center Working Paper no. 102 (2018).
4. Neil Fligstein and Doug McAdam, "Toward a General Theory of Strategic Action Fields," *Sociological Theory* 29, no. 1 (2011): 6, https://doi.org/10.1111/j.1467-9558.2010.01385.x.

CHAPTER 3

1. Neil Fligstein and Doug McAdam, "Toward a General Theory of Strategic Action Fields," *Sociological Theory* 29, no. 1 (2011): 1–26, https://doi.org/10.1111/j.1467-9558.2010.01385.x.

CHAPTER 5

1. Thomas R. Bailey, Shanna S. Jaggars, and Davis Jenkins, *Redesigning America's Community Colleges: A Clearer Path to Student Success* (Cambridge, MA: Harvard University Press, 2015); James E. Rosenbaum, Regina Deil-Amen, and Ann E. Person, *After Admission: From College Access to College Success* (New York: Russell Sage Foundation, 2007); Judith Scott-Clayton, "The

Shapeless River: Does a Lack of Structure Inhibit Students' Progress at Community Colleges?" (CCRC working paper no. 25, New York: Columbia University, 2011), https://files.eric.ed.gov/fulltext/ED515131.pdf.

2. Scott-Clayton, "Shapeless River."
3. Bailey, Jaggars, and Jenkins, *Redesigning America's Community Colleges*; Thomas R. Bailey, Shanna S. Jaggars, and Davis Jenkins, *What We Know About Guided Pathways* (CCRC research overview, March 2015), file:///Users/ls37982/Downloads/What-We-Know-Guided-Pathways.pdf.
4. Pamela Herd and Donald P. Moynihan, *Administrative Burden: Policymaking by Other Means* (New York: Russell Sage Foundation, 2018).
5. Eric P. Bettinger and Rachel B. Baker, "The Effects of Student Coaching: An Evaluation of a Randomized Experiment in Student Advising," *Educational Evaluation and Policy Analysis* 36, no. 1 (2014): 3–19, https://doi.org/10.3102/0162373713500523; Benjamin L. Castleman, *The 160-Character Solution: How Text Messaging and Other Behavioral Strategies Can Improve Education* (Baltimore: Johns Hopkins University Press, 2015).
6. Texas Higher Education Coordinating Board, "SB25 Recommended Course Sequencing Webinar" (Austin, TX: THECB, July 15, 2021), https://reportcenter.highered.texas.gov/training-materials/sb25-recommended-course-sequence-webinar-slides-july-2021/.
7. John Fink and Davis Jenkins, "Takes Two to Tango: Essential Practices of Highly Effective Transfer Partnerships," *Community College Review* 45, no. 4 (2017): 294–310, https://doi.org/10.1177/0091552117724512; Michelle Hodara, Mary Martinez-Wenzl, David Stevens, and Christopher Mazzeo, "Exploring Credit Mobility and Major-Specific Pathways: A Policy Analysis and Student Perspective on Community College to University Transfer," *Community College Review* 45, no. 4 (2017): 331–49, https://doi.org/10.1177/0091552117724197.
8. Alfred Herrera and Dimpal Jain, "Building a Transfer-Receptive Culture at Four-Year Institutions," *New Directions for Higher Education* 2013, no. 162 (2013): 51–59, https://doi

.org/10.1002/he.20056; Alicia C. Dowd, John J. Cheslock, and Tatiana Melguizo, "Transfer Access from Community Colleges and the Distribution of Elite Higher Education," *Journal of Higher Education* 79, no. 4 (2008), 442–72, https://doi.org/10.1353/jhe.0.0010.

9. Peter Riley Bahr, "Cooling Out in the Community College: What Is the Effect of Academic Advising on Students' Chances of Success?," *Research in Higher Education* 49, no. 8 (2008): 704–32, https://doi.org/10.1007/s11162-008-9100-0; Melinda Mechur Karp, Lauren O'Gara, and Katherine L. Hughes, "Do Support Services at Community Colleges Encourage Success or Reproduce Disadvantage? An Exploratory Study of Students in Two Community Colleges" (CCRC working paper no. 10, New York: Columbia University, 2008), https://files.eric.ed.gov/fulltext/ED499920.pdf.
10. Debra D. Bragg, "How Transfer Partnerships Support More Equitable Baccalaureate Attainment," *New Directions for Community Colleges*, no. 192 (2020): 11–19, https://doi.org/10.1002/cc.20419; Joshua Wyner, K. C. Deane, Davis Jenkins, and John Fink, *The Transfer Playbook: Essential Practices for Two-and Four-Year Colleges* (Aspen Institute and Community College Research Center, 2016), https://www.sanjac.edu/sites/default/files/transfer-playbook.pdf; Theresa Ling Yeh and Lia Wetzstein, "A Continuum of Transfer Partnerships: Toward Intentional Collaborations to Improve Transfer Outcomes," *New Directions for Community Colleges*, no. 192 (2020): 21–35, https://doi.org/10.1002/cc.20420.
11. Robert Kelchen, *Higher Education Accountability* (Baltimore: John Hopkins University Press, 2018); Adrianna Kezar and Daniel Maxey, "Understanding Key Stakeholder Belief Systems or Institutional Logics Related to Non-Tenure-Track Faculty and the Changing Professoriate," *Teachers College Record* 116, no. 10 (2014): 1–42, https://doi.org/10.1177/016146811411601007.

APPENDIX

1. Texas Higher Education Coordinating Board, "Institutional Resumes" (Austin, TX: THECB, 2017), http://www.thecb.state.tx.us/apps/resumes/.
2. Authors' calculations using state administrative data obtained from the Texas Education Research Center.
3. Texas Higher Education Coordinating Board, "Institutional Resumes."
4. Authors' calculations using state administrative data obtained from the Texas Education Research Center.
5. Neil Fligstein and Doug McAdam, "Toward a General Theory of Strategic Action Fields," *Sociological Theory* 29, no. 1 (2011): 1–26, https://doi.org/10.1111/j.1467-9558.2010.01385.x.
6. Matthew B. Miles and A. Michael Huberman, *Qualitative Data Analysis: An Expanded Sourcebook* (Thousand Oaks, CA: Sage, 1994).

ACKNOWLEDGMENTS

This six-year project came to fruition by merging our interests from research projects focused on community college transfer that were initially funded by the Greater Texas Foundation's Faculty Fellows program. Through the foundation's continued funding, we were ultimately able to continue following students over time, turning what was originally proposed as a two-year study into a six-year study. Without the generous support of the Greater Texas Foundation, we would not have been able to build this rich understanding of the complex web of actors shaping community college transfer.

The project relied on a lot of labor beyond our own. We are also indebted to the many graduate research assistants who worked to conduct interviews throughout the study, forging relationships with the students and maintaining contact over the years. We want to thank Sherri Castillo, Andrene Castro, Ashli Duncan-Buchanan, Wes Edwards, Eliza Epstein, Marisol Garza, Catherine Hartman, Saralyn McKinnon-Crowley, Joanna Sanchez, Carmen Serrata, Lauren Shook, and Elif Yücel. We thank Uri Treisman for encouraging us to pursue funding for this research and supporting our efforts to move the research forward. We also want to thank three anonymous reviewers who offered feedback on our book proposal and helped us refine our arguments, in addition to countless other reviewers who have offered feedback on manuscripts that also draw from our longitudinal qualitative data set, which helped us to build toward the ideas in this book. We also want to thank Jayne Fargnoli, our editor at HEP, for her patience as we faced delays in moving the project forward—babies, pandemics, and competing career obligations—and to Joanie Eppinga, our thoughtful external copyeditor, whose feedback encourages us to clarify our writing. Additionally, we are grateful to our wonderful colleagues at the University of Texas at Austin, who supported both of us as early career scholars, helping us carve out the space for a long-term research project like this one.

ABOUT THE AUTHORS

Lauren Schudde is an associate professor of educational leadership and policy in the College of Education at the University of Texas at Austin. She studies how to ameliorate social inequities in the United States through higher education policy. Because the majority of college students, particularly those from low-income families, attend broad-access institutions, her research prioritizes students and policies at community colleges and regional public universities. Schudde received her PhD in sociology from the University of Wisconsin–Madison. Prior to joining the faculty at the University of Texas, she was a postdoctoral fellow at the Community College Research Center at Teachers College, Columbia University.

Huriya Jabbar is an associate professor of education policy in the Rossier School of Education at the University of Southern California. Her research uses sociological and critical theories to examine how political and structural forces shape how policies and reforms are implemented within organizations, and how that ultimately influences opportunity, inequality, and democracy in preschool, K–12, and higher education systems in the United States. Before joining the faculty at the University of Southern California, Jabbar was an associate professor at the University of Texas at Austin. She received her PhD in the Policy, Organizations, Measurement, and Evaluation program from the School of Education at the University of California, Berkeley.

INDEX

admissions, 1, 32–33, 65–66, 125, 126–127
  bilateral agreements on, 54
  to flagship universities, 45–46, 47, 59–60, 70
  of freshman, 55–56
  gatekeeping in, 58–62
  governance units in, 39, 58
  incumbent influence on, 37
application process, 32–33
articulation agreements, 19
  bilateral, 7–8, 42, 53–54
  challengers on, 75, 76–77
  general or generic, 72
  statewide, 7, 10, 11, 13, 30, 124
associate degree, 8, 9, 70, 114, 124, 125, 126, 127
autonomy, institutional, 5, 7, 8, 10, 12, 14, 122
  in core curriculum, 47–53
  of flagship universities, 19, 47–53
  state policies on, 33–34, 42, 67
bachelor's degree, 3, 4, 7, 23
  associate degree credit transfer to, 9, 125, 126, 127
  diversion from, 4, 25–27
  time to earn, 2, 9, 14
biases, 15
bilateral transfer agreements, 7–8, 42, 53–54

California, 10, 125, 126
capital, 14, 28
certificate programs, 26
challenger role, 37, 40, 62–67
  in community colleges, 19, 40, 73–80
common course numbering, 8, 30, 75, 76, 79, 123
community college staff, 16–17, 29–30, 69–89
  accuracy of information from, 2, 71, 87–88, 96–97
  as challengers, 19, 40, 73–80
  diversion by, 4, 25–27
  in field approach, 40–41, 43

- community college staff (cont.)
  - hesitant advisees of, 101–104, 114
  - as implementers, 19–20, 40, 73–74, 79–84
  - intrusive advising by, 29, 122
  - practice recommendations on, 127–129
  - and system trusters, 104–108, 114
- cooling out ambitions, 4, 25, 26
- core-complete status, 48, 50, 64, 71, 72
- core curriculum, 6–7, 11, 30, 42, 123
  - challengers on, 64
  - at flagship universities, 48–53, 61–62
  - transfer guides on, 57
- coursework, 2, 6, 52, 123
  - admissions personnel on, 59–60
  - common numbering of, 8, 30, 75, 76, 79, 123
  - core curriculum in. *See* core curriculum
  - equivalent. *See* equivalency in coursework
  - in hidden curriculum, 27–31
  - instructional quality in, 15
  - policy recommendations on, 124–127
  - prospective institution on, 65
  - transfer guides on. *See* transfer guides
  - transparency on, 122–123, 130–131
  - in two plus two systems, 34
- credit transfer, 6, 12, 13–14
  - accountability in, 124, 125
  - advocacy on, 71–72, 73
  - agreements on. *See* articulation agreements
  - in associate degree, 9, 125, 126, 127
  - challengers on, 64, 74–79
  - of core curriculum, 6–7, 30, 48–51, 123
  - course numbering system in, 8, 30, 123
  - as elective credit, 49, 84
  - Field of Study on, 49–53
  - hidden curriculum for, 27–31
  - implementer role in, 80–84
  - information gathering on. *See* information gathering
  - number of, 72, 80
  - recommendations on, 124–127
  - reforms on, 122–124
  - reverse, 8
  - at transfer-receptive institutions, 65–66
  - transparency in, 122–123, 130–131
  - Tuning Texas on, 51–53
  - university decisions on, 27, 31–33, 51–57, 83–84, 119
- cultural capital, 28

- decentralized systems, 9–10, 12, 71, 88–89
  - autonomy in, 7, 42

student responsibilities in, 12, 20, 42, 92, 116
transfer agreements in, 7, 11, 42
disconnected students, 95–96, 108–112, 114–115, 128–129
diversionary processes, 4, 25–27
diversity and equity, 126, 130, 132

elective credits, 49, 84, 109, 125
emerging research universities, 46, 49, 53, 55, 63, 65
enrollment management, 32, 55, 60
equivalency in coursework, 8, 12, 47, 51, 55
student knowledge on, 56, 60, 61, 65
transfer guides on, 12, 64–65, 79
websites on, 64–65, 83–84

Field of Study, 49–53, 123
field perspective, 4, 24, 25, 35–43
challengers in, 19, 63, 73
disconnected students in, 108, 114
flagship universities in, 39, 47, 58, 59
governance units in, 39, 67
hesitant advisees in, 104
implementers in, 19, 20, 40, 73, 93–94, 113
incumbents in, 39, 67
interaction of multiple organizations in, 5, 14, 17–18, 33, 35, 131
policy and practice implications of, 20–21, 117–132
resource curators in, 100, 114
strategic action fields in, 18, 36–37, 40, 73
transfer agreements in, 54
view of transfer problem in, 17, 21, 88, 119
first-generation college students, 61, 78, 91, 101–102, 105
flagship universities, 18, 19
admission to, 45–46, 47, 59–60, 70
autonomy of, 19, 47–53
challengers in, 66–67
Field of Study in, 49–53
incumbents in, 39, 47, 58, 59
power and influence of, 46, 47–54, 72
transfer guides of, 56–59, 64

gatekeeping, 15, 58–62, 130
governance units, 37, 39, 58, 67
Guided Pathways, 118, 121

hesitant advisees, 95, 101–104, 114, 115, 128
hidden curriculum, 27–31

implementers, 37, 40
community college staff as, 19–20, 40, 73–74, 79–84
students as, 20, 40, 73–74, 91–116
incumbents, role of, 37, 39, 40, 47, 58, 59, 67

information gathering, 20, 91–119, 120, 125
accuracy in, 28, 82, 87–88, 97
barriers to, 13–14, 86–87
on course equivalency, 64–65, 83–84
decentralization affecting, 20, 92, 116
from destination university, 58–61, 62
by disconnected students, 95–96, 108–112, 114–115, 128–129
by first-generation college students, 61, 91, 101–102, 105
by hesitant advisees, 95, 101–104, 114, 115, 128
on hidden curriculum, 27–31
by misinformed or underinformed, 92, 94–95, 104, 107, 112
policy reforms on, 122–123
by resource curators, 42, 59, 61, 92, 95, 96–100, 114, 115
responsibility for, 84–88
strategic action fields in, 36
by system trusters, 95, 104–108, 114, 115
at transfer events, 69–71, 128
from transfer guides. *See* transfer guides
triangulation strategy in, 61, 92–93, 96, 97, 98, 100, 113
trust but verify in, 61
from trusted others, 14, 29
from websites, 13, 14, 30, 62, 64–65, 83–84, 92
interviews, 16–17, 136–146
with staff, 16–17, 18–19, 46–47, 74
with students, 16, 20, 91
intrusive advising, 29, 122

major of study, 9, 48–53, 81
associate degree in, 9, 11, 125
core curriculum in, 2, 7, 72, 92
faculty decisions on credits in, 32, 51–53, 54, 55–56, 59, 61, 84
Field of Study on, 49–53, 123
information gathering on, 97, 100, 107, 108, 109
transfer guides on, 57, 58, 60, 86

noninclusive selective universities, 15, 32, 39, 45–62

Ohio, 7
organizational approach, 4, 5, 18, 35
field level in, 35–43

power dynamics, 5, 35, 70, 72, 77, 83–84, 119–120
flagship universities in, 47–62, 72
strategic action fields in, 37, 40, 41
public higher education system, 5–13
decentralized, 9–10, 11, 12, 20, 42, 88

diversity and equity in, 126, 130, 132
power and politics in, 77
transfer issues as problem of, 17, 21, 119

regional comprehensive universities, 18, 46–47, 61–62, 64–65
challengers in, 66, 78
on transfer agreements, 52
on transfer guides, 56–57
research methods, 16–17, 133–146
resource curators, 42, 59, 61, 92, 95, 96–100, 114, 115
reverse credit transfer, 8

social capital, 14, 28
state policies, 5–13, 20–21, 30–31, 131–132
on core curriculum, 6–7, 11, 30, 42, 48–51, 64, 123
on course numbering, 8, 30, 123
Field of Study in, 49–53
on institutional autonomy, 33–34, 42, 67
recommendations on, 124–127
reforms of, 121–124
Texas Transfer Framework in, 52, 123, 124, 127
transfer agreements in, 7–8, 10, 11, 30, 53–54, 72
Tuning Texas in, 51–53
university influence on, 19, 46, 47–54, 119–120
strategic action fields, 18, 36–37, 40, 73
structuralist theories, 14, 25, 26–27, 29, 33, 131
students, transfer-intending, 1–5, 29–30
compared to freshman students, 46, 55–56
core-complete status of, 48, 50, 64, 71, 72
diversion of, 4, 25–27
earning bachelor's degree, 2, 4, 9, 14, 23, 26
as first-generation in college, 61, 78, 91, 101–102, 105
information gathering by. *See* information gathering
interviews with, 16, 20, 91, 136–141
misconceptions about, 32, 66, 132
rate of transfer, 3, 11, 100, 104, 108, 112, 115
in strategic action fields, 40–42, 43
system trusters, 95, 104–108, 114, 115

Texas A&M University at College Station, 46, 51, 59, 109, 127
Texas Higher Education Coordinating Board, 10, 52
Texas Transfer Framework, 52, 123, 124, 127
transfer guides, 29, 52, 86

on course equivalency, 12, 64–65, 79
of flagship universities, 56–59, 64
major-specific, 57, 58, 97
as student responsibility, 60, 62, 81
transfer-receptive institutions, 32, 58, 126–127, 129
challengers in, 62–67
Tuning Texas, 51–53
two plus two system, 7, 12, 34

universities
accountability of, 124, 125
application to, 32–33
autonomy of. *See* autonomy, institutional
challenger role in, 40, 62–67
in credit transfer decisions, 27, 31–33, 51–57, 83–84, 119
diversity and equity in, 126, 130, 132
enrollment management in, 32, 55, 60
flagship. *See* flagship universities
gatekeeping at, 15, 58–62, 130
governance units in, 39
incumbent role in, 39, 47
information barriers of, 13–14, 86–87
interviews with staff in, 16–17, 18–19, 46–47
noninclusive selective, 15, 32, 39, 45–62
power and influence of, 31–33, 35, 46, 47–54, 72
practice recommendations on, 129–131
transfer guides of. *See* transfer guides
transfer-receptive, 32, 58, 62–67, 126–127, 129
University of Texas at Austin, 45–46, 51, 59, 126–127

Wang, Xueli, 27
website resources, 13, 14, 30, 62, 92
on course equivalency, 64–65, 83–84